Reinventing Ritual

Reinventing Ritual

CONTEMPORARY ART AND DESIGN FOR JEWISH LIFE

DANIEL BELASCO

WITH CONTRIBUTIONS BY
ARNOLD M. EISEN
JULIE LASKY
TAMAR RUBIN
DANYA RUTTENBERG

The Jewish Museum, New York
Under the auspices of the Jewish
Theological Seminary of America

Yale University Press
New Haven and London

This book has been published in conjunction with the exhibition *Reinventing Ritual: Contemporary Art and Design for Jewish Life*, organized by The Jewish Museum.

The Jewish Museum, New York
September 13, 2009–February 7, 2010

Contemporary Jewish Museum, San Francisco
April 22–September 28, 2010

The Jewish Museum
Director of Publications: Michael Sittenfeld
Curatorial Publications Coordinator: Jenny Werbell
Text edited by Michael Sittenfeld and Jenny Werbell

Yale University Press
Publisher, Art and Architecture: Patricia Fidler
Senior Editor, Art and Architecture: Michelle Komie
Manuscript Editor: Laura Jones Dooley
Production Manager: Mary Mayer
Photo Editor: John Long

Designed by Emily Lessard
Set in Flembo, Leitura, and National type
Printed in China by Kwong Fat

The Jewish Museum
1109 Fifth Avenue
New York, New York 10128
thejewishmuseum.org

Yale University Press
P.O. Box 209040
New Haven, Connecticut 06520-9040
yalebooks.com

Library of Congress Cataloging-in-Publication Data

Belasco, Daniel, 1975-
   Reinventing ritual : contemporary art and design for Jewish life / Daniel Belasco ; with contributions by Arnold M. Eisen . . . [et al.].
     p. cm.
   Published in conjunction with an exhibition held Sept. 13, 2009-Feb. 7, 2010, the Jewish Museum, New York, and Apr. 22-Sept. 28, 2010, Contemporary Jewish Museum, San Francisco.
   Includes bibliographical references and index.
   ISBN 978-0-300-14682-0 (Paperbound : flexicover)
   1. Jewish art and symbolism--Exhibitions. 2. Art, Jewish--20th century--Exhibitions. 3. Art, Jewish--21st century--Exhibitions. 4. Judaism--Liturgical objects--Exhibitions. 5. Judaism--Customs and practices--Exhibitions.
   N7414.75.N48 2009
   704.094896--dc22
2009011043

A catalogue record for this book is available from the British Library.

The paper in this book meets the guidelines for permanence and durability of the Committee on Production Guidelines for Book Longevity of the Council on Library Resources.

10 9 8 7 6 5 4 3 2 1

Front cover: Studio Armadillo: Hadas Kruk (Israeli, b. 1970) and Anat Stein (Israeli, b. 1972), *Hevruta-Mituta*, 2007. Plastic chess board, thirty-two knitted skullcaps, 2 3/8 x 27 1/2 x 27 1/2 in. (6 x 70 x 70 cm). Courtesy of the artists

Back cover: Talila Abraham (Israeli, b. 1965), *Dantela*, 2004. Stainless steel: etching, 5 x 13 x 13 in. (12.7 x 33 x 33 cm) Courtesy of the artist, Kfar Truman, Israel.

Contents

DONORS TO THE EXHIBITION   VI

JOAN ROSENBAUM
FOREWORD   VII

ARNOLD M. EISEN
PREFACE   XI

DANIEL BELASCO
Chopping Noodles   1
The Art of Jewish Practice

JULIE LASKY
"How Can I Simply Throw Away These   47
Shoes That Have Served Me So Well?"
Recycling and Jewish Ritual

DANYA RUTTENBERG
Heaven and Earth   71
Some Notes on New Jewish Ritual

TAMAR RUBIN
A Cultural Timeline, 1994–2008   94

EXHIBITION CHECKLIST   104

NOTES   110

BIBLIOGRAPHY   119

CONTRIBUTORS   125

ACKNOWLEDGMENTS   127

INDEX   131

THE JEWISH MUSEUM BOARD OF TRUSTEES   138

Donors to the Exhibition

Reinventing Ritual: Contemporary Art and Design for Jewish Life is made possible through the generosity of the Andrea and Charles Bronfman Philanthropies, the Leir Charitable Foundations, and the Joyce and Irving Goldman Family Foundation. Additional support was provided through the Melva Bucksbaum Fund for Contemporary Art.

Foreword

AS THE LARGEST AND OLDEST ART MUSEUM IN THE UNITED STATES presenting Jewish culture, The Jewish Museum holds a position of preeminence in a number of areas. One is the role of a world leader in the creation, exhibition, and interpretation of contemporary Jewish ritual objects. The exhibition and catalogue *Reinventing Ritual: Contemporary Art and Design for Jewish Life* is at once the latest iteration of the Museum's ongoing commitment to the intersection of art, design, and Judaism and the consummation of a decade of commissions, acquisitions, and study that have redefined the field of Judaica. This redefinition springs from an expansion of collecting criteria to include objects for newly created ceremonies as well as conceptual artworks that expand awareness of Jewish practice.

Ritual objects have long been fundamental to the study of Jewish aesthetic expression and material culture. Indeed, The Jewish Museum itself was created as a collection of historical ritual objects set apart from the books and manuscripts of the library of the Jewish Theological Seminary in 1904.

The Museum began to create major exhibitions of contemporary Judaica shortly after its move to the Warburg mansion in the late 1940s as part of a larger commitment to art of the present. In 1956, one year before the landmark exhibition *Artists of the New York School: Second Generation,* the first museum show of the next wave of Abstract Expressionists, the Museum established an artist-in-residence program called the Tobe Pascher Workshop, where artists pioneered modernist ritual objects for homes and synagogues. Lasting for more than thirty years, the Workshop was nurtured by Museum patrons Vera List and Abram Kanof and directed first by the extraordinary Bauhaus-influenced designer Ludwig Wolpert and later by his student, the masterful Moshe Zabari, both of whom had one-person exhibitions at the Museum. Vera List also supported an annual graphic program that engaged notable contemporary artists in creating a multiple work in honor of the Jewish New Year.

Simultaneous with an efflorescence of experimentation in the art world from the late 1950s through the 1960s, new American design and architecture exerted a deep influence on the construction of synagogues and creation of ritual objects. All of this was reflected in the Museum's programs and exhibitions, which included five shows in a ten-year period focusing on ceremonial objects and synagogue design, notably *Recent American Synagogue Architecture* organized by Richard Meier in 1963.

Synagogues and Jewish ceremony also inspired an enormously varied group of installations or small one-person exhibitions during the 1980s and 1990s. Frank Stella's *Polish Wooden Synagogues: Constructions from the 1970s* was shown in 1983. In 1995, an exhibition of Louis Goodman's design for Temple Israel in Greenfield, Massachusetts, further reflected the influence of the historical Polish synagogues. Two sukkahs, one architectural by Allan Wexler and another painterly by Eli Content, were exhibited in 1988. In 1990, the *mikvah* (ritual bath) was the subject of the Israeli artist Oswaldo Romberg's installation *The Last Mikvah on Fifth Avenue*—a work perceived as being both inside and outside the Museum. The mikvah was also the subject of Shari Rothfarb's *Water Rites*—a sculpture and video installation exhibited in 1999, the same year in which the Museum featured an installation of Sophie Calle's *The Eruv of Jerusalem*.

Following the closure of the Tobe Pascher Workshop in the late 1980s, the Museum began to engage a new roster of international artists with an ongoing series of commissions to create Jewish ritual objects in a range of materials and styles. In 1993, Artes Magnus worked with the Museum to develop a silver-and-gold seder plate by the sculptor Tom Otterness. In more recent years, in particular as the Museum marked its centennial in 2004, the Henry J. Leir Curator generated several new commissions—single works and multiples—thus adding a new body of work to the collection and expanding the availability of exceptional pieces for sale in the Museum's shop. Among the projects have been Karim Rashid's silicone Hanukkah lamp (2004), Lyn Godley's sculptural Hanukkah light installation (2004), a spice container by Chunghi Choo (2004), suites of silver objects by Adam Tihany (2004) and Lella Vignelli (2007), and a group of mezuzahs by Allan Wexler (2006).

The 1990s also saw the initiation of two important programs directed at engaging a larger group of artists in the process of considering the intersection of art and Jewish ceremony. *The Hanukkah Project,* which has also been called *Light x Eight,* was supported by a gift from Trustee Barbara Horowitz and has become a biannual exhibition of contemporary artists working with various aspects of light. From Olafur Eliasson's installation in front of our building in 1998 to Julianne Swartz's interactive light vessels in 2008, more than thirty artists have installed pieces throughout the Museum—in galleries, windows, hallways, and the permanent exhibition.

A second program evolved from a gift in 2006 from the Henry J. Leir Foundation, which funded a curatorial position whose mandate was to focus even greater attention on the development of contemporary ceremonial art for exhibition and collection. In particular, this gift provided the wherewithal for the Museum's staff and its Contemporary Judaica Acquisitions Committee to create a more robust commissions program. The first Leir Curator was Fred Wasserman, and now Daniel Belasco occupies the position. Both have worked closely with Life Trustee Stuart Silver, who has nurtured all aspects of the contemporary Judaica program through his position as Chair of the Contemporary Judaica Acquisitions Committee.

I extend my gratitude to all of those trustees and curators—past and present—whose vision, gifts, and talent have allowed the Museum to stay current with the creativity of artists, designers, and architects working in the field of Jewish ceremony. Special thanks to Daniel Belasco for his thoughtful and creative direction of this project. His selection of works for *Reinventing Ritual* reflects a time of immense inventiveness and vitality in the exploration of Jewish ritual as a means to find meaning in a complex world. I commend the authors of this volume for their lively, thought-provoking contributions, which shed new light on contemporary Jewish ritual art and its makers. Finally, I wish to express my deep gratitude to The Jewish Museum Board of Trustees for its unwavering generosity and encouragement, to the members of the Contemporary Judaica Acquisitions Committee for their dedication and counsel, and to the Henry J. Leir Foundation for its indispensable support of this project.

JOAN ROSENBAUM
Helen Goldsmith Menschel Director
THE JEWISH MUSEUM

Preface

RITUAL HAS MADE A COMEBACK OF LATE. AFTER DECADES (INDEED, centuries) of denigration in the West as behavior that is hopelessly stereotyped, formulaic, repetitive, and largely boring, after unceasing put-down as rote action that stifles creativity and innovation, or as legalism that inhibits genuine feeling, or as mere "ritualism" that stands in the way of true human relationship and blocks the way to authentic encounter with God—after all of that, we find ourselves in 2009 at a moment when ritual is once again receiving its due as an essential element of culture.

Thank goodness. I don't know what I would do *without* ritual, whether in my friendships, my community, or my attempts to fill my space and time on earth with sacredness and meaning. The older I get, the more I appreciate ritual performances and forms. Of course these run the risk of decline into thoughtless habit, mere routine. That is the occupational hazard of ritual, so to speak. But without the motions that ritual imposes and prescribes, I would not know moments of fulfillment that I treasure almost as much as love and life itself.

Consider: How can we communicate what is most important without resort to words and gestures that we did not ourselves invent? (Greeting cards and birthday celebrations come to mind.)

How can we maintain relationships, convey the respect we owe one another, or maintain a proper sense of the life passages we share without marking significant moments with respectful, affectionate pause? (Spouses are right to be upset at forgotten anniversaries. A Rosh Hashanah or Shabbat ignored is a missed opportunity for focus and renewal.)

How can we join in community with strangers or people well known to us, act in concert with them for the good, or go deeper into life together if we do not gather around the same table at a specific time (a seder, say), move to the same rhythms (a wedding hora, for example), respond to the same image and symbols (a Hanukkah menorah), and take for granted—so as to challenge!—the same rules and expectations?

We realize as we grow into life that it, like friendship and religion, is a lot more art than science—and we learn, as we grow with art, that it depends for its most vital performances on form. What dancer, actor, painter, or musician does not find freedom and creativity inside the bounds of discipline and craft? What Jew is not uplifted by particular melodies, holidays, images, liturgies—and commands?

Jews have long created sacred space and marked sacred time with ritual forms and objects designed to order, beautify, set apart, and ennoble. The need to express gratitude to God for blessings received, dangers averted, or the gift of life itself is as old as humanity, according to the Torah. The desire to invest this expression with creativity and exceptional craft likewise seems to have animated our ancestors as much as it motivates us. Think of the wisdom poured into the design and construction of the Tabernacle and its appurtenances—or the simple act of *chanting* Torah rather than merely reading it, of *parading* around the sanctuary rather than merely walking or sitting in place, or the *art of the silversmith* that has for many centuries heightened every ceremony of the Sabbath. Contemporary artists stand in a long tradition when they find new means of expressing ancient human longings and directing Jewish worship, emotion, and attention to the Most High.

This is a wonderful time to be a Jew, not only because of the rights and opportunities we enjoy in America and elsewhere—opportunities denied to almost all our ancestors—and the palpable blessing of being alive at the same time as the reborn state of Israel. We have in addition the chance—as many of our ancestors did not—to encounter Jewish tradition on its own terms, as it were. We approach Bible and Talmud, Sabbath and festivals, unencumbered by a priori dismissals of "religion" or "tradition" or "mere ritual." Students in university or adult education classrooms have the pleasure of renewed appreciation of the Torah, unperturbed that it does not proceed systematically, unafraid of internal contradictions as the text moves from one genre to another without pause. Parents aware of how messy life is, or citizens inured to societal and political imperfection, read Torah or the rabbis with new understanding. Judaism has always prized ritual perfection (a goal attainable, if we work at it) as a guide and means to ethical achievement (always far more elusive). Modern self-consciousness about all this enhances rather than precludes appreciation of Judaism as it does Jewish art. The abiding chutzpah of Judaism—its central claim that the world is not good enough and that we can make it and ourselves better, with God's help—imperceptibly inspires contemporary Jewish creativity and performance.

I am repeatedly inspired by the number, range, and quality of the artists who are drawn to work inside centuries-old Jewish forms. Delve into the works featured in *Reinventing Ritual* and you cannot help but reflect on the many ways in which contemporary artists in a variety of media have both adopted and challenged received religious conventions. They have labored long and hard in silver and concrete, photo and montage, oil and ink to endow ritual performance and religious commandment with new beauty and meaning. The action here belongs to both the ritual *and* the art. So too the form. We leave the works in the exhibition thinking harder, seeing differently, pondering what we have been missing until now, and appreciating yet again the power and beauty stored up in Jewish tradition. We also are likely to emerge duly disturbed by what we have seen and experienced—exactly how we leave a ritual moment that succeeds in its intention to jar, arrest, humble, and enlighten us.

The Jewish Theological Seminary has long promoted the kind of devotion to Jewish tradition that involves an open mind, a willing heart, and the conviction that the life of Torah grows from what we bring to it as full members of contemporary society and culture. May we observe, enhance, rethink, reinvent, renew, and rededicate Jewish art and ritual for many years to come.

ARNOLD M. EISEN
Chancellor
THE JEWISH THEOLOGICAL SEMINARY

My products reflect the desire to preserve the special and personal touch that was an integral part of all handcrafted objects designed in the past. The products fill a need, and a yearning, for original hand-made objects, which, despite the use of industrial materials and technology, arouse nostalgia. In the transition from the "language" and texture of fabric to the stiffness of stainless steel, I try to preserve an art form that is constantly losing its significance in today's world.

— TALILA ABRAHAM

TALILA ABRAHAM
(Israeli, b. 1965)
Dantela, 2004
Stainless steel: etching, 5 x 13 x 13 in.
(12.7 x 33 x 33 cm)
Courtesy of the artist, Kfar Truman, Israel

DANIEL BELASCO

Chopping Noodles

THE ART OF JEWISH PRACTICE

MUSING ON THE QUESTION OF WHETHER THERE IS A "JEWISH ART,"
Harold Rosenberg identified an "underground" of Jewish object-making that
by the 1960s was all but lost.[1] The critic fondly recalled his grandfather, a
shochet and mohel, designing and casting lead dreidels and assembling hard
pastries in the form of toy furniture. And his grandmother baked challah
in the shape of birds and crafted the thinnest of noodles. "Nobody ever
thought of my grandfather as an artist," Rosenberg wrote. However tied to
the past, the work of his grandparents might be art "if you wish to consider
chopping noodles a Jewish art form," he mused.[2] Rosenberg quickly dropped
the subject and turned to evaluate in greater detail the commonly recognized
examples of Jewish visual creativity of the 1960s, such as the "metaphysical Judaica" of Yaakov Agam and Ben Shahn and the individualist expression
of Mark Rothko and Barnett Newman. But the question of whether chopping noodles is Jewish art remained unresolved, as Rosenberg never took a
stand, passing the verdict on to future generations.[3]

Rosenberg—the great critic of action painting as authentic source
of modern art based on individual self-expression, which flowed directly
from French existentialism mixed with his notion of American "coonskin"
resourcefulness—did not perceive that the creative actions of his elders
and ancestors would later inspire the current developments of Jewish visual
expression.[4] Just a few years after Rosenberg's query, a young group of

1

FIG. 1. Directions to braid challah into a bird, from Richard Siegel, Michael Strassfeld, and Sharon Strassfeld, eds., *The Jewish Catalog: A Do-It-Yourself Kit* (Philadelphia: Jewish Publication Society of America, 1973). Illustrations by Stu Copans. Photograph by Richard Goodbody

countercultural Jews tapped into the deep underground of Jewish creativity and tradition as a source for contemporary revitalization of Jewish practice. The landmark publication *The Jewish Catalog: A Do-It-Yourself Kit* (1973) included a recipe, and pictorial step-by-step instructions, for how to make a bird-shaped challah (FIG. 1).[5]

Myriad social and aesthetic developments in the past four decades have resulted in the acceptance of the making of the stuff of life as art. Today, some of the major innovations in art have transformed derided and neglected practices of "handicrafts" (Rosenberg's term) into conceptual strategies and critical content. With the benefit of retrospect, Rosenberg's notion of action can be recuperated and deployed in a different way. To identify contemporary Jewish art and design, one can first identify *what a Jewish action is.* From this perspective, chopping noodles takes on entirely new significance.

JEWISH ACTION

One way of defining Jewish action is ritual. Ritual is formalized and symbolic performance, already close to art. "Ritual is an act or actions intentionally conducted by a group of people employing one or more symbols in a repetitive, formal, precise, highly stylized fashion. Action is indicated because rituals persuade the body first; behaviors precede emotions in the participants," wrote Barbara G. Myerhoff.[6] In this essay I build on the ideas of Myerhoff and contribute an aesthetic evaluation of Jewish ritual to include those actions that are performed in the practice of Judaism: observance of the commandments in the Torah, celebration of holidays, rites of passage, and other organized means of transmitting Jewish mores, law, and knowledge. New rituals like same-sex weddings, the reclaiming of *mikvah*, and *simchat bat* (naming ceremonies for newborn girls) draw from the well of thousands of years of tradition. By this measure, all Jewish ritual is ancient and contemporary, familiar and radical.

Vanessa Ochs, a scholar of new Jewish ritual objects, follows the anthropological perspective that ritual is inherently creative, not divinely ordained.[7] This definition challenges the traditional views of Jewish practice, which assert a hierarchy, placing the timeless Torah and its text-related objects and rituals at the center and culturally specific ceremonial practices at the periphery.[8] An expanded and nonhierarchical view of Jewish ritual is composed of scores of specific actions: eating, drinking, counting, smelling, lighting candles, praying—physical acts that serve a larger symbolic or legal matrix. These verbs, these actions of identity, constitute the systems of exchange that modulate difference and embodied subjectivity. Jewish ritual practice, or "Jewish action," does not only link us to a remote divinity, but is embedded in everyday life, providing a wealth of meaningful forms and materials that formalize transitions, enhance ethical awareness, link past to present, negotiate politics and authority, and trigger ethnic pride. The power of ritual is its special metaphorical resonance that produces meaning in transformations of contemporary life.

Certainly there is extreme variation in the practice of Jewish ritual in time, space, and community. Yet in reaction to the pervasiveness of consumer culture, artists today are using the essential things that all humans share—food, adornment, and the environment—as the materials of art. Because these commonalities are patterned and structured according to ritual and religious codes with symbolic and mythic resonance, artists wishing to discover deeper values and authentic experience in the every-day have renewed interest in traditional faiths. Many works, structured by direct and immediate exchanges and relations among people, objects, and experiences, create a small space of spiritual presence within the impersonal consumer lifestyle.

In charting the turn toward everyday ritual as art, a useful current theory is "relational aesthetics," coined by critic and curator Nicolas Bourriaud in the 1990s. Relational aesthetics describes the emergence of a preponderance of new artworks involving social actions: cooking a meal, shopping, engaging in small-scale transactions. Bourriaud has written, "Meetings, encounters, events, various types of collaboration between people, games, festivals, and places of conviviality, in a word all manner of encounter and relational invention thus represent, today, aesthetic objects likely to be looked at as such, with pictures and sculptures regarded here merely as specific cases of a production of forms with something other than a simple aesthetic consumption in mind."[9] The objects, performances, and spaces of encounter are opportunities to rethink interaction, connection, and integration. Art today encompasses the aestheticization of the structures and systems that modulate the relationships between people.

These relations and their material and performative expression are especially formalized through religious and secular ritual. The notion of "Jewish action" presents ritual as an open system. Contemporary artists focus on Judaism as a lived, organic experience, not one fixed in text or custom, by identifying the physical acts that embody rituals and removing them from their familiar or unspoken position to bestow new meanings. They disconnect the actions of ritual from their symbolic intent and re-purpose them for unexpected connections and harmonies. The results of the process are hybrid objects that blend the new and traditional, art and craft, sacred and profane, irony and sincerity, offering both artist and viewer an opportunity for contemplation and critique.

BOP KABBALAH AND OTHER PRECURSORS

The emergence of Jewish ritual action as a medium of art, or a subject or form of art, gained momentum in the United States in the 1950s, a period when Beat poetry, John Cage, and neo-Dada expanded art to include anything.[10] The heterogeneity and combativeness of "bop kabbalah," in the phrasing of Allen Ginsberg's epic poem *Howl* (1956),[11] ran against the utopian ideals of modernist abstraction, which were imported into syna-gogue architecture, Judaica design, and liturgical music in the 1950s.[12]

The technique is well described by Marjorie Perloff: "Ginsberg's syntax typically puts parts of speech into 'incorrect' slots so as to make us rethink their relationship."[13] More than mere collage or juxtaposition, Ginsberg's work was a radical reimagining of the sacred content of the speech act itself while retaining fragmentary signs of its sources in Judaism.

In a similar manner, Wallace Berman began to apply Hebrew letters, especially *aleph*, on a range of materials, such as parch-ment, wood assemblage, his loose-leaf journal *Semina*, and photographs of artist Jay

FIG. 2. Wallace Berman (American, 1926–1976), *Untitled*, 1956–57. Collage on canvas: ink and shellac on torn parchment paper on primed canvas, 19 ½ x 19 ½ in. (49.5 x 49.5 cm). The Menil Collection, Houston, on loan at Ackland Art Museum

DeFeo posing nude in front of her painted masterwork, *The Rose* (1958). The letters had "no specific, translatable sense," Berman said.[14] Berman's one-person show in Los Angeles in 1957 exhibited ritualistic works that lacked the usual irony and pop cultural references of his other work, instead presenting a commingling of religious symbolism and constructions of the divine in art and love (**FIG. 2**). *Panel* jumbled words and letters in Yiddish and Latin pasted on a wood stele or altarpiece with a single wing.

A mysterious structure, titled *Temple*, enclosed a robed figure with its back to the viewer. "Berman's assertion of the centrality and power of religious imagery and ritual had the same kind of impact that blasphemy once did," wrote Rebecca Solnit.[15] The sacredness of the letters among the funk and the junk of West Coast art endowed sexual liberation and hipster rebellion with a Jewish romanticism. Berman's use of Hebrew along with Christian forms sought to reenchant the everyday, operating on a spiritual plane inspired by Kabbalah to critique contemporary society.[16]

Allan Kaprow indicated that elements of Jewish ritual were on his mind as he began to develop his forms and theories of Happenings. His first Environment at the Hansa Gallery, in 1958, included music, staged performances, and, according to the artist, "sections of slashed and daubed enamel and pieces of colored cloth hung in bands that looked like Jewish prayer shawls or other ceremonial adornments."[17] Enshrouded, visitors experienced a disorienting atmosphere that broke down the usual boundaries between art and the individual (**FIG. 3**). Kaprow said, "I immediately saw that every visitor to the Environment was part of it."[18] Kaprow

(top) **FIG. 3. Allan Kaprow in his first Environment in March 1958 at the Hansa Gallery**. Research Library, The Getty Research Institute, Los Angeles (980063). Photograph by Francesco Cantarella

(bottom) **FIG. 4. Barnett Newman (American, 1905–1970),** *Second Station,* **1958**. Magna on canvas, 78 1/8 x 60 5/16 in. (198.4 x 153.2 cm). National Gallery of Art, Washington, D.C., Robert and Jane Meyerhoff Collection. © 2009 The Barnett Newman Foundation/Artists Rights Society (ARS), New York

FIG. 5. **Allen Ginsberg and Jack Kerouac speaking at the Hansa Gallery on March 16, 1959.** Photographed by Fred W. McDarrah, Premium Archive Collection, Getty Images

infused the immediate experience of Jewish prayer into the work of art, while at the same time he questioned the psychological grip of Jewish nostalgia and memory in mixed-media assemblages like *Grandma's Boy* (1957). He anticipated the negative reactions of critics expecting the autonomy of modern art. For them, the presence of religious ritual, which demands communal participation, broke the rules. Critic John Canaday compared the spare black-on-white "zips" of Barnett Newman's painting series *Stations of the Cross* (1958-66; FIG. 4) to "unraveled phylacteries."[19] A student of Jewish mysticism, Newman wrote a letter to the *New York Times* accusing Canaday of anti-Semitism, an indication of how Jewish ritual objects became contentious as both source and sign of radical art in America in the late 1950s.

For Kaprow, Environments and Happenings were distinctly *not* religious rituals but highly personal experiences: "Naturally, ritualism is not ritual, and it was evident to all that what we were doing was an invention, an interlude, coming not out of belief and custom but out of the artist."[20] This applies to Allen Ginsberg as well. His poetry played freely with the action of ritual as material for declarative poetry, remixing Jewish ritual into incantations against contemporary postwar consumer culture. Ginsberg wrote *Kaddish* (1957-60) to both memorialize his mother and address his conflicted feelings about the place of Jewishness in America (FIG. 5). "Naomi's death made me remember my own generation, and how it must pass," Ginsberg wrote his grandmother.[21] Ginsberg dislodges the process of mourning from the self-referential symbolism of religion and opens it to the secular and the vernacular.

The Jewish countercultural movement of the late 1960s injected the avant-garde creativity of Kaprow and Ginsberg into Jewish communal practices, developing the nonhierarchical *havurah* movement (Havurat Shalom was founded in Boston in 1968) and politically conscious Passover celebrations (the first Freedom Seder was held in Philadelphia in 1969).

FIG. 6. **Sheila Benow** (American, b. 1939), *The Happening*, 1967. Temple Beth El, Spring Valley, New York. Collection of Rabbi and Cantor Frishman. Photograph by Robert Lieberman. This painting depicts the "art service," or religious "happening," held in 1967 at Temple Beth El.

The first Jewish congregation in the United States to integrate the avant-garde into synagogue rituals may have been a Shabbat "art service" at Temple Beth El in Spring Valley, New York, in July 1967. The Friday evening included a sermon on universality by John Cage, new liturgical and abstract music composed by Gershon Kingsley and LaMonte Young, dancing by Frances Alenikoff and Laura Forman, strobe lights, taped electronic sound, and film projections.[22] The event was recorded in a spontaneous, on-the-spot painting by Sheila Benow (FIG. 6).

The kinesthetic experience, grafted to the traditional Kabbalat Shabbat service, showed how art can make faith physical. "A service such as this makes people re-interpret the words of the service. The dance represents a sermon in sight and sound," the temple's rabbi Louis Frishman said at the time.[23] The convergence of the expanded notions of art and the practice of Jewish ritual has only become more widespread. Judaism is a ritualistic religion, so anyone who wants to change it has to work with the forms of ritual.

If women have been marginal in the narrative thus far, the second half of the story is theirs. The greatest source of new ritual practices in the past forty years has been feminism, which has transformed Judaism to integrate women in old rituals and validate women's long-standing practices. A disembodied masculine faith has been replaced by an embodied Judaism inclusive of all genders. Women have reclaimed ancient rituals of tefillin, mikvah, and rabbinical thought while inventing new objects, symbols, and liturgy. Also influential have been the joyous and communal rituals of Hasidism, popularized by Rabbi Shlomo Carlebach and the Chabad movement. Both feminism and Hasidism, despite their divergent politics, view Judaism as action. This notion has taken on force in recent years, as Judith Plaskow has proposed, in an ethics based on "our bodies as the foundation of our being."[24] In this view, the body is the prime locus of religious experience.

Jewish scholars and activists across the spectrum have noted
the new consensus that Jewish identity and spirituality is profoundly
expressed through physical practices.[25] Historian Jonathan D. Sarna has
said, "There is a difference between being Jewish and doing Jewish;
it's the doing that leads to understanding."[26] The Reform movement is
revitalizing rituals once discarded, while Orthodox communities are
embracing feminism and social justice as never before, both pivoting on
the axis of action. According to Jewish Theological Seminary chancellor
Arnold M. Eisen, the practice and observance of a wide range of rituals
has surpassed the profession of belief in shaping communal identity and
individual sense of self.[27]

EXHIBITION AS RITUAL

Reinventing Ritual focuses on rendering into form the physical actions
required in the performance of Jewish ritual. The art can be made by
Jews and non-Jews, so long as the work itself participates in or comments
on Jewish ritual. Just as menorahs and synagogues may be crafted or
designed by non-Jews, so may actions be performed by nonbelievers while
retaining their formal integrity as functionally Jewish. Indeed, the
practice of Jewish rituals now extends beyond the Jewish community in the
United States in the form of secular mezuzahs and Christian Passover
seders. The splitting of ritual from functionality makes it more visible and
open to reinvention on a formal and structural level. Included in this
exhibition are not only examples of Jewish ritual objects made in contemporary styles and materials, but also conceptual works that use the
forms and symbols of ritual to comment on daily life and identity.

A goal of this exhibition is to propose conceptual and aesthetic
terms for the explosion of new Jewish rituals, art, and objects that
has occurred since the mid-1990s. This period is defined by the urge to
discover first premises—the roots and ruptures—when ritual could
be radical. "We need to be lean: Our rituals have to be stark, exposed,
stripped to the bone. That's what makes them accessible," writes
Rabbi Niles Goldstein.[28] "By locating the translations that were made in
the myth and ritual, we can discover what it is that makes this holiday
[Purim] quintessentially Jewish," writes Douglas Rushkoff.[29] By taking
Jewish action or ritual practice as the central metaphor, we can begin
to trace how artists are steadily dismantling the modernist hierarchies of

high and low in art and of sacredness in Judaica. This exhibition
sharpens the notion of "post-identity" art by, in the case of Jewish culture,
focusing on the externalized and shared acts of ritual.[30] The common
aesthetic strategy of "post-identity" art is that the artists privilege, sometimes to the point of abstraction, the bare facts and primary sources
of culturally specific materials and performances.

The ability to take fragments from previously incommensurate
categories and seamlessly blend them in a new whole is one of the most
important aesthetic aspects of the work selected for *Reinventing Ritual.*
Contemporary artists are exhausted by the constant and unresolvable
psychological tensions created by ongoing ideological debates that force
one to choose one side or the other. Artists today want to be able to
select aspects of both that they identify with and are not willing to
sacrifice their values for the sake of purity. In trying to solve the problem
of finding a third way, artists have focused on craftsmanship. By purpose-
fully and conscientiously analyzing the properties of different forms, artists
craft a new unity from the best elements of two or more competing
alternatives.

The process of reinventing ritual requires integration and connection by questioning the politics of practice. If postmodernism was about
deconstruction, then our time is about reconstruction. The contemporary
impulse is exemplified by Sandi Simcha Dubowski's documentary film
Trembling before G–d (2001), which argued that one can be both gay and
Orthodox and documented the struggles of men and women trying, in
their individual ways, to make peace with the tensions between the two
identities.[31] Or Azra Akšamija's *Frontier Vest* (2006; FIG. 7), a hybrid ritual
object imbued with the utopian dream that the shared act of faith offers
protection. In response to the Israeli-Palestinian conflict, Akšamija designed a Kevlar flak jacket that can be reshaped in a variety of covers to be
used in Jewish and Muslim prayer, evoking the individual's place in diverse
communities. Many works in *Reinventing Ritual* are the outcome of similar
struggles to seek unity in fragmentation.

The artworks in *Reinventing Ritual* are grouped in four thematic
nodes based on the specific actions that create dynamic relationships
among individual, community, and environment. The nodes are organized
around four verbs: covering, absorbing, building, and thinking. These
categories were selected to be both precise and poetic, demonstrating how

FIG. 7. Azra Akšamija (Austrian, b. Bosnia and Herzegovina, 1976), *Frontier Vest*, 2006. Kevlar and mixed media. Courtesy of the artist

specific mechanics of ritual are reinvented in a range of both related and disparate forms and materials. The phenomenology of ritual is emphasized in these categories over traditional symbolism and meaning. Many works in this exhibition are functional objects that could be used in conventional Jewish ritual or ceremonial practice while offering an artistic commentary on injustice and consumer culture. Other conceptual art-works employ the forms, structures, and symbols of Jewish ritual to critique contemporary beliefs and practices. All share a commitment to environ-mentalism, biopolitics, or social justice. Ritual artworks are self-critical catalysts for religious, social, and cultural awareness and change. The new art emphasizes functionality and tangibility to call attention to and ultimately question the way we live our lives.

COVERING

Ritual sacralizes the everyday through the separation of sacred from profane. The act of covering performs that task by inserting a layer to create categories and distinctions. The concept of distinction is central to Jewish spirituality. Covering is especially important in the marking of difference in bodies.[32] Clothing marks the varying roles of the sexes in traditional Judaism and regulates attitudes toward modesty and public displays of sexuality. Garments also indicate rites of passage and transitions from one phase of life to another. Clothing may also mark the difference between Jews and others. The covering of objects in Jewish ritual—such as challah, the bread eaten during Sabbath, and the Torah itself—serves to sanctify the object and add ceremonial drama to its unveiling and presentation for ritual use. These rituals date back to the original Tabernacle, where the holiest of holies was screened by a curtain. By covering, truth or essence becomes contingent on exterior presentation.

A central ritual of covering involves the act of prayer. When praying, Jews—traditionally men but increasingly women as well—will wear a tallit, or shawl, a garment with four corners, each bearing the tzitzit, or fringes, required by law. The act of covering oneself during prayer creates a personal space that focuses the mind and spirit and marks the participant as part of a holy community. Rachel Kanter's prayer shawl, *Fringed Garment* (2005; p. 77), addresses the traditional separation of the sexes by combining a kitchen apron and traditional prayer shawl, fusing the female and male roles—the domestic and the sacred—into a new gestalt. The work is a neat design solution to the contemporary problem of a woman who prays in synagogue and also looks after her small children, and therefore needs a more functional, closer-fitting garment that fulfills the dual responsibilities of prayer and childcare.[33] Formally, it is more inventive than a feminized prayer shawl woven in pink or decorated with images of the matriarchs. The best new ritual objects have reimagined the structure of ritual garments in order to recalibrate the vocabulary of distinction.[34]

Tefillin, the phylacteries containing tiny parchment scrolls worn in daily prayer, with their black leather straps graphically wound up the forearm, have become a powerful symbol for contemporary artists exploring

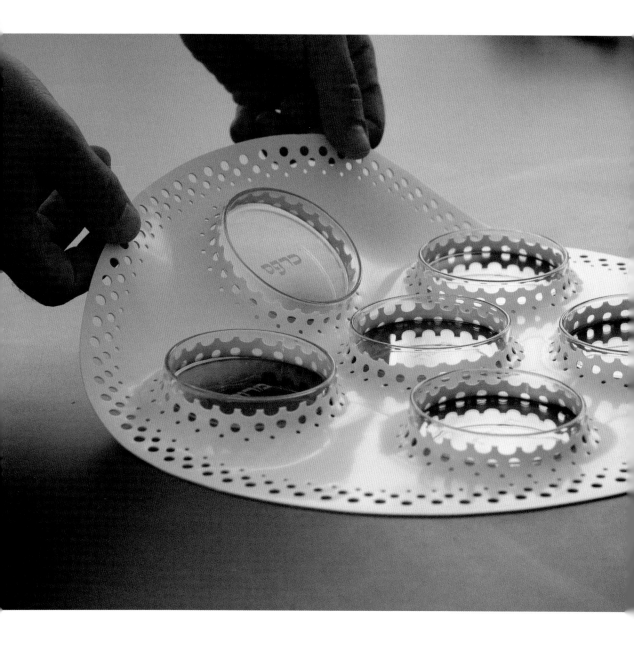

SAHAR BATSRY
(Israeli, b. 1974)
Volcano Seder Plate, 2008
Glass, silicone, ¹/₂ x 12 in.
(1.5 x 32 cm)
Courtesy of the artist, Tel Aviv

Volcano is a unique seder plate made of delicate glass plates set in a specially treated silicone sheet resembling a traditional white tablecloth. The names of Passover's symbolic foods are laser engraved onto the glass plates. Silicone, usually associated with everyday use, gets a glamorous, festive, and delicate look. Playfully abolishing the distinction between tablecloth and dish, the pattern holds the glass plates structurally, thanks to the elastic quality of the material. Volcano questions the function of holiday items, "high" and "low" quality materials, and the use of ornaments in contemporary Judaica.
— SAHAR BATSRY

the (gendered) body in Jewish ritual. The artist duo LoVid represents
tefillin symbolically as a continuous electrical signal linking the spiritual
community to God and the generations. Their sculpture *Retzuot
(ShinShinAgam)* (2008; p. 78), not meant to be worn, reconstitutes the
elements of tefillin as live abstract video and exposed circuit boards
connected by wires wrapped in a colorful cotton patchwork. The meanings
of the covenantal words from the Torah, covered by the boxes, are exposed
in an aesthetic that fuses art and engineering, intuition and knowledge.

     If Kanter considers the act of covering an opportunity for a new
identity across gender or religious divisions, then other artists explore the
diversity within one side of the divide. The video and performance artist
Oreet Ashery looks toward a masculine world with wonder and trepidation.
The artist posed as a man to infiltrate a mass religious pilgrimage to Mount
Meron on the holiday Lag b'Omer. Once the subversion of cross-dressing is
accepted, her video *Dancing with Men* (2003, re-edited 2008; p. 90) becomes
less about her transgression and more a documentation of the variety of
music and fashion, from Hasidic to reggae to hip-hop, among the participants enacting the ritual of pilgrimage. Ashery, the consummate outsider,
scrupulously observes the encoded distinctions.

     Because covering is such a central part of Jewish ritual, a number
of artists have examined the practice from a completely different direction
to call attention to the relation of the decorative and the functional in
Jewish domestic rituals. Two Israeli designers took lace, a common ornament
on Israeli tabletops and other furniture, and turned it into a commercially
manufactured ritual object suffused with the memory of past Israeli taste.
Talila Abraham's *Dantela* (2004) is an etched steel basket designed to
hold a stack of square *matzot* for the holiday of Passover. The artist's line of
MetalaceArt products blends the contrasting properties of steel and
lace into a new expression, restoring the anonymous female craftsperson to
contemporary Israeli life. Another designer, Sahar Batsry, rendered lace in
another unexpected material, silicone, in his *Volcano Seder Plate* (2008). The
soft material, gripping six small glass dishes in place, requires a flat surface
for support, and thus this cover/container transforms the entire table into
a "plate" supporting the symbolic foods blessed and consumed during the
Passover ritual meal.

     The works in the category "Covering" rethink the garments,
textiles, and other apparatus worn, draped, or wrapped in the performance

of Jewish ritual. In these works, difference is the start of a conversation about the presence and histories of the body.

ABSORBING

Covering is a culturally contingent set of actions that relates to external rituals of separation. The internal process of absorbing can be considered the inverse, as it relates to the permeation of boundaries. Absorption, a natural course of action, is necessary for creating and sustaining life. As such, Jewish law and ritual regulates what, when, and how one thing may be absorbed into another. This can range from eating and drinking to menstruation and sex. Acts of absorption threaten to violate the borders constructed for *kedushah* (holiness) and are the most visceral and private of rituals. Ritual objects powerfully frame and present the substances to be absorbed. The works selected in this category scrutinize the symbolic systems deployed in Jewish ritual and culture in general to maintain health and well-being.

The production, transportation, and preparation of food have become a leading area of the expanded consciousness of the ethics and meanings of Jewish practice in the past several decades. The Jewish laws require the separation of milk from meat, ritually prescribed slaughter methods, and the avoidance of some foods entirely. New Jewish environmentalist organizations like Hekhsher Tzedek and Hazon work to bring social ethics into Jewish observance and ritual in farming, land use, consumer goods, and animal slaughter, which has supplanted vegetarianism as the locus of new ritual activism.[35] The video *If This Is Kosher . . .* (2006), narrated by the writer Jonathan Safran Foer for the Web site Humane Kosher, helped expose the violent slaughter of animals in the AgriProcessors plant in Postville, Iowa. As the federal raid on the world's largest *glatt* kosher plant in 2008 demonstrated, the actual practice of Jewish ritual slaughter does not guarantee ethical treatment of either animals or workers.

Food itself has become a major medium and subject of art. Tamara Kostianovsky's *Unearthed* (2007), a life-size sculpture of a slaughtered cow rendered in the artist's clothes with uncanny craftsmanship, forces the viewer to ruminate on the interconnections of the human body, the treatment of animals, national identity, and ritual. The tension between covering and absorbing is best captured in this work, where clothes, the markers of culture and style, appear as bone and sinew. We lose ourselves in

15

My wishbone is an artifact of the chicken, a memento of a
dinner, and a symbol of my family's history of chicken
farming and chicken cooking. I used a lost-wax casting
process to turn the wishbone from a 2004 family
dinner—featuring roast chicken and a round table of
grandparents, parents, siblings, and cousins—into a metal
replica of the event. This wishbone transcends that specific
family dinner and represents family dinners and family in
general. By wearing my wishbone, others can reflect on
their own associations of the significance of the wishbone.

—ALEXIS CANTER

ALEXIS CANTER
(American, b. 1981)
Wishbone, 2004
14K gold, 1¹/₂ x 1 in. (3.8 x 2.5 cm)
Courtesy of the artist,
Cambridge, Massachusetts

*Because one aspect of kosher slaughter emphasizes
the need to avoid unnecessary suffering of the animal,
I am interested through my work in examining the
awareness of a moral responsibility involved in the act
of killing. In my artwork the "clothed" cows represent
the flesh—animal and most certainly human. My hope is
that the reflection and careful examination of the act
of animal killing will instill a visceral empathy that will
in turn make us question current military approaches,
social injustices, and the way "fleshy clothed bodies"
are treated around the world.*

— TAMARA KOSTIANOVSKY

TAMARA KOSTIANOVSKY
(Argentinean, b. Israel 1974)
Unearthed, 2007
Clothing, embroidery thread,
metal hooks, 91 x 29 x 33 in.
(231.1 x 73.7 x 83.8 cm)
Courtesy of Black and White Gallery,
New York

The plates serve the rabbinical dietary law that ordains two sets
    of dishes, one each for milk and for meat, derived from the
    biblical commandment "You shall not cook a kid in its mother's
    milk" (Exodus 23:19, 34:26, Deuteronomy 14:21). Instead of
    inscribing the words "milk" and "meat" on the different plates
    (the established distinction code), I preferred to describe
    "milky" and "meaty" through visual content and form. Milk/Meat
    Couples suggests that practicing the separation of foods
    heightens our awareness and capacity of distinction. Electric
    Blue/Shocking Pink visually represents the pig (the taboo)
    from the fact that neither the Bible nor the oral law forbids its
    visual representation. This set doesn't suggest eating the
    pig. Rather, it challenges our excessive fear of transgression.

— RACHEL MOSES

RACHEL MOSES
(Israeli, b. France 1963)
Electric Blue/Shocking Pink, from
Dairy and Meat Dishes, 2004/2008
Two plates, 10 ½ in. diameter (26.7 cm)
Pencil and watercolor transfer on
porcelain plates
Courtesy of the artist, Paris
A registered design patent, Rachel
Moses 2004, 2008

BOTTOM
Milk/Meat Couples, from *Dairy and
Meat Dishes*, 2004/2008
Two plates, 10 ½ in. diameter (26.7 cm)
Pencil and watercolor transfer on
porcelain plates
Courtesy of the artist, Paris
A registered design patent, Rachel
Moses 2004, 2008

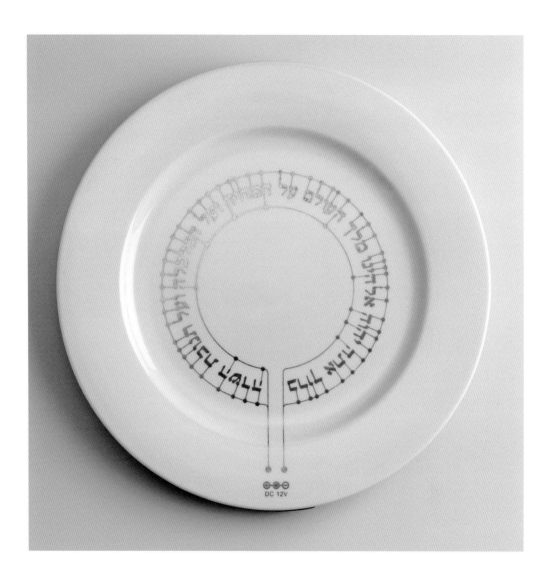

This conceptual mock-up uses the conductive properties
of silk-screened gold, or amorphic metal films
printed in the same manner, as for use in circuit
boards and car windshield defrosters. Hook up
the plate to an electrical source, and the current
will run through the "decoration," thereby keeping foodstuffs warm. A graphic connection becomes
evident as the electric wire-letter welding
points mimic the quill typography in the Jewish
Holy Scriptures. Thus, ornate graphic patterns
are bestowed "function" in the most modernist
sense of the word.

— AMI DRACH AND DOV GANCHROW

AMI DRACH
(Israeli, b. 1963) and
DOV GANCHROW
(Israeli, b. United States 1970)
+/- Hotplate, 2003
Readymade plate, silk-screened
conductive print, abs connector
housing, 9 in. diameter (23 cm)
Courtesy of the artists, Tel Aviv
Photograph by Moti Fishbain

Jewish custom dictates the washing of hands on waking,
    before meals, at funerals, and so on. Traditionally,
    the vessel used for this ritual washing, or netilat yadayim,
    is a cup with two handles. One hand holds one handle
    while pouring water on one's second hand. The "clean" hand
    then grasps the second handle to rinse the "first" hand.
    This two-handle typology avoids "recontamination" during
    the cleansing process. Our design was created by reexam-
    ining the ritual's objectives and constraints and was realized
    through a dialogue focusing on objects, interiors, and
    customs (Christian, Jewish, Muslim) in Arab eateries.

—DOV GANCHROW AND ZIVIA

DOV GANCHROW
(Israeli, b. United States 1970) and
ZIVIA
(Israeli, b. 1960)
Netilat Yadayim (Hand Cleansing
Vessel), 2008
Cast ceramic, 15 ¾ x 6 in. diameter
(40 x 15 cm)
Courtesy of Loushy Art & Projects,
Tel Aviv
Photograph by Moti Fishbain

The seder plate consists of a tray and six elevated plates of wood. The seder plate performs the expression of "lifting and saying" (magbiha ve omer) and relates to the custom of lifting and discussing the symbolic foods, a practice that appears again and again in the Haggadah.

— STUDIO ARMADILLO

STUDIO ARMADILLO:
HADAS KRUK
(Israeli, b. 1970) and
ANAT STEIN
(Israeli, b. 1972)
Seder Plate, 2005
Wood, acrylic, 15 ³/₄ x 18 ¹/₂ in.
(40 x 47 cm)
Courtesy of the artists, Tel Aviv

the animal, so a new level of empathy is triggered, more profound than simple anthropomorphism or analogy.

The ritualized consumption of food plays a powerful role in Jewish memory. Alexis Canter's family ran a kosher chicken farm in New Hampshire. As part of her practice in turning what she calls "organic remnants" into fine jewelry, Canter has cast hundreds of pendants from the wishbones of chickens and Cornish hens mailed to her by relatives around the country. Though not a ritual object per se, Canter's pendants function as a token of contemporary Jewish identity rooted in ritual practice, updating the *chai* (Hebrew for "life," often displayed on necklaces), mezuzah, and Star of David and their more traditional sources in language, text, and symbolism. Michael Rakowitz's ongoing performance project, *Enemy Kitchen*, teaches groups how to cook Iraqi food, the cuisine of his Jewish family. The project is an example of the current trend in aestheticizing folk cultures to resist the false dichotomies of politics. There is a shared sensibility between the two artists, as Rakowitz and his wife, the critic Lori Waxman, commissioned Canter to create their wedding bands, which were cast in silver from frozen calamari rings. To use *traif* (forbidden food) to symbolize marriage is a surprising gesture of the fluidity of contemporary Jewish identity.

In thinking about how rituals structure eating, containers and utensils are abundant sources for creativity. Plates, which function as both vessels for food and surfaces for design, have become an especially important medium in recent years. Sets of plates for separating milk and meat by Rachel Moses (2004/2008) use contemporary graphics to explore centuries of interpretation as well as fulfill the ritual function of separation.[36] Ami Drach and Dov Ganchrow's *+/– Hotplate* (2003) also involves a stenciled plate, but with a heat-conductive print. The Hebrew inscription is the blessing said after a meal (or snack) when bread was not eaten. The lettered plate adds value to the act of saying a blessing by rendering it a source of warmth, since a meal without bread lacks other rituals for food such as hand-washing and saying grace. Ganchrow collaborated with designer Zivia for their ceramic *Hand Cleansing Vessel* (designed 2000, cast 2008); the spouts and handles become interchangeable, representing the act of washing each hand with the other before meals. Action becomes form as well in a seder plate (2005) with six elevated dishes designed by Studio Armadillo to concretize the act of

The havdalah *ritual is the Threshold Zone where we*
we pause to gather up our gift of creation—
that we ourselves are empowered creators—
and prepare to reenter the everyday from
the Sabbath. Rested, we have become alert.
We look around; we sniff. We will step out
to seek nature's robust world filled with order,
surprises, danger, strangeness. For one last
moment, we dip our heads deep into the scents
of creation; we are mesmerized, enlivened.
In our Scent Garden, *we want to show how*
brilliant and interesting nature is. We think
learning is part of gorgeousness.

— MIERLE LADERMAN UKELES AND STEVEN N. HANDEL

MIERLE LADERMAN UKELES
(American, b. 1939) and
STEVEN N. HANDEL
(American, b. 1945)
"I'm Talking to You": A Scent
Garden: Three Different Voices
from Nature, Version II, 2009
Numbered scientific vessels of various
sizes, including petri dishes, beakers,
Erlenmeyer flasks, specimen dishes,
cylinders, and volumetric flasks,
and containing spices, fruits, leaves,
roots, grasses, fragrant oils, seeds,
flowers, herbs, and photographs;
mirrored glass base, acrylic texts, list,
diagram, and key, 15 ¾ x 24 x 24 in.
(40 x 61 x 61 cm)
Commissioned by The Jewish Museum,
New York

lifting each symbolic food as the reader of the Haggadah explains its significance during the seder.

Another way of internalizing nature is through smell. Fragrant spices are blessed and inhaled as part of the *havdalah* ceremony, which marks the bittersweet closure of the weekly Sabbath. Mierle Laderman Ukeles reinvents the typical spice container by transforming it into an exegesis of the act of smelling. Working in collaboration with Steven N. Handel, a professor of ecology, Ukeles classified the types of scents found in nature and the purpose they serve as the interchange among species of the plant and animal worlds. Some scents attract (roses entice bees to pollinate and reciprocate with nectar), some repel (spices like cinnamon taste bitter), and some seduce (orchards entice bugs without giving them anything). As author Michael Pollan puts it, "All these plants, which I'd always regarded as the objects of my desire, were also, I realized, subjects, acting on me, getting me to do things for them they couldn't do for themselves."[37] New Jewish rituals of absorption take into account the subjectivity of the natural world. Absorption is not a one-way street.

Marriage is a potent metaphor of absorbing separate subjectivities into a new, singular union. There has been an explosion of new rituals relating to marriage to accommodate a range of differences, from same-sex to feminist to interfaith, reinforcing the centrality of marriage in Jewish life.[38] All use different means to work toward the goal of unification. One of the most powerful metaphors in Judaism is that the Torah is the marriage of God and the Jewish people. Our experience of art, as well, can be considered a marriage, suggested Mark Rothko and Adolph Gottlieb: the meaning of a work of art "must come out of a consummated experience between picture and onlooker."[39] Contemporary artists, concerned with the intimate fusion of marriage, isolate the specific rituals that unite the lives and fates of two individuals.

Bruria Avidan designed a *Wedding Cup* (2004) for the modern wedding ceremony in which two cups of wine are blessed and consumed. Each partner joins the halves of a silver cup, made watertight with a silicone ring and rubber binders. Inspired by the double-stacked cups popular in eighteenth-century Germany, Avidan's work takes advantage of new technology to produce an object that elegantly combines ritual function and form. Another wedding ritual is the consecration of one partner to the other through the exchange of rings. The spoken names of the married

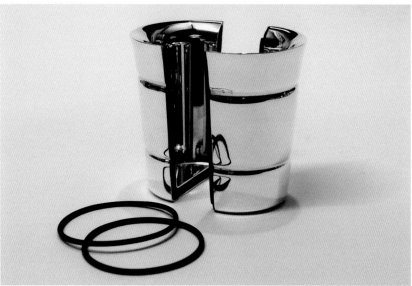

This unique wine cup is designed for use under the marriage canopy
at the Jewish wedding ceremony. It concretizes the main
idea of Jewish marriage, binding two who come together to form
a single whole, symbolizing becoming part of the couple
relationship to establish a Jewish household and family. The
silver cup comes in two parts: the bride and groom can
each bring one half of the cup. The two halves are then bound
together in one cup and filled with wine for the recitation
of the Seven Blessings of the wedding ceremony.

— BRURIA AVIDAN

BRURIA AVIDAN
(Israeli, b. 1966)
Wedding Cup, 2004
Silver, silicone, rubber
3 $^5/_{16}$ x 2 $^3/_4$ in. (8.5 x 7 cm)
Courtesy of the artist, Har Adar, Israel

This ketubah *was commissioned for the wedding of close friends who are performance artists, working a great deal with sound. The groom grew up in New York, and the bride is from Tel Aviv. I recorded the bride and groom saying each other's names and translated that, using computer software, into a waveform. I then carved by hand a linoleum stamp of each waveform image, which I used to make the print. The background pattern is a bathymetric map of the ocean between New York and Tel Aviv. The ocean connects their pasts, being the route between them and the gulf they crossed to meet.*

— TRACY ROLLING

TRACY ROLLING
(American, b. 1972)
Ketubah for Tali and Kyle, 2001
Linoleum print, painting, and
silk-screen on paper, 14 x 22 in.
(35.6 x 55.9 cm)
Courtesy of Tali Hinkis and Kyle
Lapidus, New York

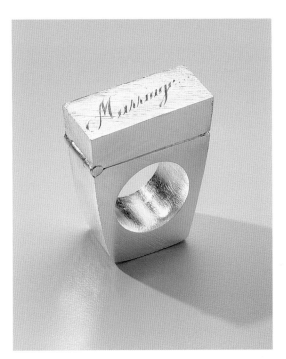

"Marriage, I would rather have a cup of tea!" is based on a corruption of Boy George's remark, "Sex, I'd rather have a cup of tea." It is a statement on the agunot, *or chained women, who are trapped by the laws designed to protect them. The idea is to subvert the traditional marriage ring, showing, on the outside, glossy and engraved perfection and, on the inside, a more scarred and imperfect interior. The cup of tea in question sits on the family table, stating that there is always a choice. The alternative of a life without marriage is viable and free.*

— MILA TANYA GRIEBEL

MILA TANYA GRIEBEL
(British, b. 1963)
"Marriage, I would rather have a cup of tea!" 2000
Sterling silver, 1 9/16 x 1 1/4 x 9/16 in.
(4 x 3.2 x 1.4 cm)
The Jewish Museum, Purchase:
Contemporary Judaica Acquisitions
Committee Fund and Hyman and
Miriam Silver Fund for Contemporary
Judaica, 2008-153

artists called LoVid, Tali Hinkis and Kyle Lapidus, were recorded and
the sound waves were printed in a simple bar graph. Tracy Rolling then
rendered the graphs in a colorful linoleum print for their marriage
contract, *Ketubah for Tali and Kyle* (2001), which captures the absorption of
marriage through speaking and listening. A more critical piece on the
limits of Jewish marriage laws was made by Mila Tanya Griebel, in *"Marriage,
I would rather have a cup of tea!"* (2000). Calling attention to *agunot*, or
women bound to husbands who refuse to grant them a divorce in Jewish law,
Griebel riffs on a laconic quotation from the pop singer Boy George to
comment on the condition of the isolated woman. The solitary teacup questions the failure of Jewish law and custom to prevent the ritualized
processes of absorption from becoming a trap and entailing a loss of liberty.

BUILDING

The establishment of sacred space, an essential purpose of ritual, denotes
temporal boundaries and establishes a sanctified setting. In *The Sabbath:
Its Meaning for Modern Man* (1951), Abraham Joshua Heschel wrote that
Jews create cathedrals in time, as opposed to a brick-and-mortar house of
worship.[40] Heschel, like most Jewish modernists, privileges the abstract
over the material. His eloquent text, in elevating the status of time, under-
values the ways in which Jewish ritual requires the physical marking of
space. There is increased scholarly and creative interest in the ways Jews
create Jewish space through vernacular ritual expressions. Artists
Sophie Calle and Mark Wallinger each investigate the *eruv*, the boundary
line—often simply a wire—that creates a private space in public by Jewish
law to perform tasks during Shabbat. "For many Jews, it is primarily in the
place-bound practice of Jewish law and custom that religious meaning
resides," writes modern eruv scholar Jennifer Cousineau.[41] The group of
artists selected here is more concerned with the physical act of building,
a process-based approach focused on means, not ends. The result is for the
most part a ritual object or a work that examines the construction and
creation of space.

The cyclical act of building in Jewish ritual can be interrogated in
video. Sigalit Landau's *Day Done* (2007) turns the custom of leaving a part
of a new building unfinished in memory of the destruction of the Temple
(*zecher l'chorban*) into a work of performance art. She painted the exterior
wall of an apartment building in an industrial section of South Tel Aviv

*There was an old Diaspora tradition in
some Jewish houses, especially
when newly built, to leave a part of
an eastern wall unfinished, bare,
and without paint—in memory of
the Churban (the destruction
of the Temple) as well as the fleeing
from homeland into exile. Painting
an unfinished surface of an exterior
wall in Tel Aviv reverses this tradition
of remembering and yearning—that
is, forgetting and stagnating.*

— SIGALIT LANDAU

SIGALIT LANDAU
(Israeli, b. 1969)
Day Done, 2007
With sound work by Yarden Erez
HD-DVD, sound, 17 min., 32 sec.;
9:16 frame
Courtesy of the artist, Tel Aviv

The basic concept for this mezuzah was first
contemplated as we sat on scaffolds and
drank coffee with a Palestinian (Muslim)
contractor who was building Eran's home.
"You Jews will never calm down and
cease to see us as enemies until you finish
building your country," said Jabber to
the sounds of construction clattering in
the background. "This is why building
houses with and for the Jews interests me."
The fixation of the mezuzah marks the
final chord in building a home and marking
its Jewish ownership. This mezuzah wishes
to extend this dimension.

— ELAN LEOR AND ERAN LEDERMAN

ELAN LEOR
(Israeli, b. United States 1970) and
ERAN LEDERMAN
(Israeli, b. 1970)
Solomon, 2008
Silver-plated brass, blackened (oxidized)
sterling silver, 3 $\frac{3}{4}$ x $\frac{5}{8}$ in.
(9.5 x 1.6 cm)
Courtesy of the artists, Tel Aviv

Normally perceived as mundane, the ancient material concrete is here used to create religious artifacts. Used primarily in architecture on a large scale, concrete is introduced into the home as small, intimate objects. In the mezuzah the durable concrete cast slides over the metal parchment holder, which is mounted on the door frame. The letter shin *is recessed from the surface of the concrete. This design questions formal preconceptions about holy objects and challenges common assumptions about how they look and what materials they are made from.*

— MARIT MEISLER

MARIT MEISLER
(Israeli, b. 1974)
CeMMent Mezuzah, 2006
Concrete, nickel-plated pewter,
4 ⅝ x 1 ⅜ x ½ in. (11.8 x 3.5 x 1.3 cm)
The Jewish Museum, Purchase:
Contemporary Judaica Acquisitions
Committee Fund, 2008-143

Reform Jewish and other synagogue architecture of the postwar period embraced organic modernism as a style with abstract, free-flowing forms and, often, a decorative-patterned overlay. This disregard for convention in Reform temples is completely liberating to me. When I'm feeling constricted by pottery dogma, I think of these organic, rule-breaking structures with their organic modern vocabulary layered with pattern and decoration.

— JONATHAN ADLER

JONATHAN ADLER
(American, b. 1966)
Utopia Menorah, 2006
High-fired brown stoneware
with white glaze, 9 7/8 x 11 1/8 x
3 5/16 in. (25.1 x 28.3 x 8.4 cm)
The Jewish Museum, New York,
Purchase: Contemporary Judaica
Acquisitions Committee Fund,
2009–21

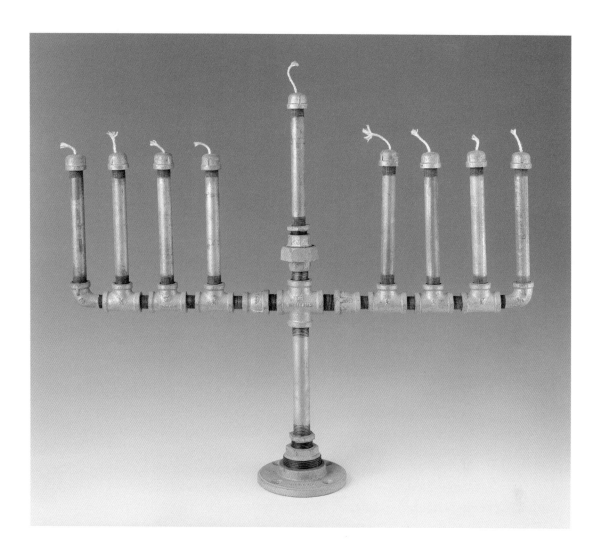

The Galvanized Steel Candelabra *is created from half-inch galvanized steel pipe fittings to form a simple and raw industrial object. The design of the menorah was a spur-of-the-moment decision. I was at Home Depot and wanted to build something fun using non-standard materials. I remember sitting in the aisle surrounded by all sorts of steel piping. An employee asked what I was building and if I needed help. I told him "A menorah for Hanukkah," and he walked away. Oh well, I figured it out on my own, anyway!*

— JOE GRAND

JOE GRAND
(American, b. 1975)
Galvanized Steel Candelabra, 2003
Steel pipe fittings, 13 x 20 ½ in.
(33 x 52.1 cm)
Courtesy of Grand Idea Studio, San Francisco

from a fixed point of a window, leaving a black mark in the hot sun. That evening her assistant repainted the "wound" a cool white, reenacting a historical pattern of destruction and repair expressed through ritual, like the customary breaking of the glass at the end of a wedding. The designers Mey Kahn and Boaz Kahn revalue destruction as creation, requiring the user to break their ceramic products—a necklace, salt and pepper shakers, and a Hanukkah lamp—in order to use them.

Artists have found the mezuzah case—which contains a scroll with a text from the Bible and is hung on the doorposts of Jewish homes as a reminder of the covenant with God—to be an especially versatile object for the demarcation of Jewish space. With the current interest in the physical actions of ritual, they are more interested in how people interact with the object than the meaning of the scroll. Elan Leor and Eran Lederman believe the most compelling aspect of the mezuzah is the instant in which it is affixed and thus designed *Solomon* (2008), which anticipates this climactic moment in its own form, that of a nail. The act of hammering the nail is more significant to a practice-based Jewish identity than the text inscribed within. Virgil Marti focused on the act of touching the mezuzah with a finger upon entry or exit and adorned his object with a model of a finger bone. *Untitled (Mezuzah)* (2007; p. 53) evokes Catholic relics or ossuaries, which include human bones as venerative or decorative materials. In Marti's impure piece, Jewish ritual finds personal metaphorical resonance with another religious tradition.

The concrete mezuzahs by Norm Paris and Marit Meisler rethink the relation between object and architecture. Paris's *Rubble Fragment 1 (Mezuzah)* (2007; p. 66) literally takes the meaning of the word *mezuzah,* or doorpost, to handcraft a tromp l'oeil architectural fragment. With its rebar and concrete, the conventional building materials of the Middle East, the work reminds us of the stakes in declaring and defending a Jewish home. Concrete as a building material is synonymous with the creation of the new Jewish state. Israeli poet Natan Alterman wrote, "We shall build you, beloved country . . . we shall clothe you in a dress of concrete and cement."[42] Israeli designer Marit Meisler departed from this notion with her set of Judaica products, including a modular Hanukkah lamp, pair of candlesticks, and hamsa ornament, all cast in her invented blend of concrete. *CeMMent Mezuzah* (2006) in particular seems inspired by the spiritual power lent to the humble material by modernist architects Louis Kahn and

Tadao Ando. When American silversmith Alix Mikesell lived in Israel in the 1990s, she frequently hunted in wrecking yards and antique shops for materials that have had "other lives."[43] She incorporated locally found plastic and rubber into her handcrafted silver mezuzahs, titled *Embrace* and *Sentinel* (both 2003; p. 67), preserving memory through material fragments and soothing the tensions between the precious and the disposable.

The menorah is another ritual object associated with architecture. A symbol of the Jewish people (it is described in the Torah and appears on the state seal of Israel), it served a vital function within the ancient Temple and contemporary synagogue, often incorporated into the decoration or structure.[44] The form of the nine-branched menorah, or Hanukkah lamp, emerged from the miracle of Hanukkah that occurred in the Temple in Jerusalem, when burning oil rededicated the Temple. Because of its close connection to reconstruction, as well as its composition of modular units, the Hanukkah lamp often inspires—and is inspired by—architecture. Potter and designer Jonathan Adler grew up in suburban New Jersey, where his first sustained exposure to modernism came through synagogue architecture. Adler told the *New York Times*, "I have always been driven by and fantasized about moving into those synagogues. They have such a groovy, brutalist, modern thing going on."[45] His glazed ceramic *Utopia Menorah* (2006) expresses the monumentality of ancient architecture blended with the baroque patterning of the organic architectural modernism of the 1960s, blending architectural monumentalism and home decor.

Engineer Joe Grand found himself on the floor of Home Depot in San Diego one December with a slew of pipe fittings spread out before him, figuring out how to construct a Hanukkah lamp for the upcoming holiday. Grand's *Galvanized Steel Candelabra* (2003) is an elegant expression of this impulse to turn the hidden materials of architecture into the stuff of ritual, a simplified version in comparison to ornate examples by R. M. Fischer and Joel Otterson. Reddish Studio similarly harmonized disparate components for its *Menorah* (2008; p. 51). The designers gathered orphaned candlesticks from flea markets and friends in Israel and assembled them into a single work, a seven-branched menorah that serves as a potent metaphor for the creation of community from mismatched components.

The works of Mikesell, Grand, and Reddish Studio connect to a long yet underappreciated history of Judaica production, the repurposing of secular and ritual materials for ceremonial or sacred use.[46] Repurposing is a hands-on process of salvaging physical and symbolic materials, exploring their metaphoric and plastic properties, and freely transferring the materials from one domain to another.[47] Harold Rosenberg mused on the power of found ritual objects in the Bible: "If you inhabit a sacred world you *find* art rather than *make* it."[48] Creativity lies in the adaptive reuse of one material or form for another, unforeseen function, which forces a reconsideration of assumptions and undermines expectations of the familiar. It is the action that lends the object power, not the other way around. The tensions between secular and sacred are neutralized in the activity of the contemporary "repurposer," who never privileges one or the other.

THINKING

Jews have long been known as the People of the Book. Rabbinical Judaism was founded after the destruction of the Temple in 70 CE, which ended cultic sacrificial rituals and established a text-based Jewish practice. Many popular images of Jews in art history portray a group of bearded men hunched over books in small rooms, or crowding around a Torah in a synagogue, as in nineteenth-century genre paintings by Maurycy Gottlieb or Isidor Kaufmann and the twentieth-century work of Max Weber. The pursuit of knowledge has never been purely cerebral. The dichotomy between the Temple Judaism of sacrifice and ritual and the Diaspora Judaism based on text and abstraction has been rethought in recent scholarship. For the rabbis who compiled the Talmud and the Mishnah, wrote Daniel Boyarin, "the human being was defined as a body."[49] Complex rituals abound in the acquisition, education, and presentation of Jewish learning. The Torah, the central text in Jewish life and the source of narrative and law, is not merely read and studied but performed and celebrated. In Judaism there has long been an understanding of the physical connection between the body and the mind, and contemporary artists explore the dynamic of embodied knowledge and thought.

Traditionally, Jews study and debate the Torah and rabbinical responses in pairs, the dialectical model eliciting deeper engagement with the arguments and evidence. Like most practices of religious education, until rather recently these schools have admitted men only. Studio Armadillo compares this activity to a chess match. The thirty-two pieces of

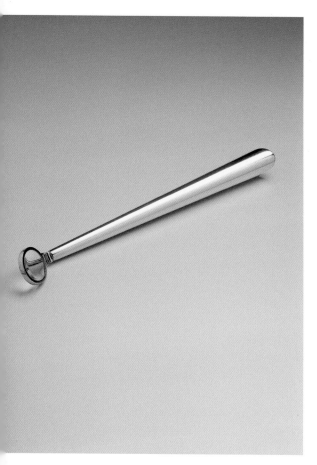

Creating contemporary Judaica allows me to examine current issues through the Jewish tradition. One format I enjoy is the yad, or Torah pointer. Octogenarian *has a magnifying glass attached to the pointing end, made to help the old rebbes read the Torah. Perhaps it can also help those people searching for something hidden within the text.* Compass *has a compass on one end. It can be a tool to help you find east (toward Jerusalem), so you know which direction to face when praying. It can also be a metaphor, referencing the Torah as a map, meant to help you find your way.*

— ANIKA SMULOVITZ

ANIKA SMULOVITZ
(American, b. 1974)
Compass, 2002
Sterling silver, compass, acrylic,
6 ¹/₂ x ⁵/₈ x ⁵/₈ in.
(16.5 x 12.7 x 12.7 cm)
The Jewish Museum, Purchase:
Contemporary Judaica Acquisitions
Committee Fund, 2008-142

LEFT
Octogenarian, 2002
Sterling silver, magnifying glass,
7 ⁷/₈ x ¹⁵/₁₆ x ⁵/₈ in.
(17.8 x 2.4 x 1.6 cm)
The Jewish Museum, Purchase:
Contemporary Judaica Acquisitions
Committee Fund, 2008-141

Hevruta—Mituta (2007; p. 83) are small, multicolored skullcaps knit by
Orthodox schoolgirls during lessons in their yeshiva. The intellectual battle
of religious education here becomes both playful and emblematic of
the steady increase of Orthodox education for women, yet the religious
identity remains marked by the style of the *kippot* (skullcaps).

Hadassa Goldvicht's video *Writing Lesson #1* (2005; p. 81) identifies a
ritual involved in Hasidic education. When a boy turns three he goes to
his first day at school, where he licks honey off letters to remind him that
learning is sweet.⁵⁰ Goldvicht, who grew up in a Hasidic community in
Israel, was not permitted to enjoy the ritual, so as an adult she devised her
own version, in which she carefully licks the Hebrew alphabet, written
in honey. The sensuality of the performance, witnessed through a translu-
cent screen, recalls the *mechitza*, which separates women from men in
Orthodox Jewish ritual. *Writing Lesson #1* both respects and probes
the boundaries of traditional Judaism, giving the corporeality of Jewish
learning a female figure.

Johanna Bresnick and Michael Cloud explore the metaphor of
learning through absorption in *From Mouth to Mouth* (2006; p. 91). They
carefully rendered a volume of the Bible into small pieces, which they then
rolled up and inserted into gel capsules. Bresnick and Cloud, along
with other contemporary artists, have used the pages of the Bible and other
religious texts as a material for plastic expression. Nechama Golan constructed a high-heeled shoe with photocopied pages from the *gemara* to make
a work critical of sexism in both the sacred and secular worlds.⁵¹ Daniel
Libeskind employed pages from the Bible as wallpaper for the interior of an
architectural model of his landmark Berlin Jewish Museum, now in the
collection of the Museum of Modern Art. This trend at once violates a taboo
against damaging any text containing the name of God, yet at the same
time treats these pages with the utmost respect, either preserving them as
art or ensuring their reverential disposal by storage in a *geniza* (text ware-
house) or burial. These artists respect the sacredness of the Bible but locate
its value in the materiality of its pages as much as the specific meaning of
its words. This shift in interest in the book from content to form is one of the
most profound phenomena of contemporary ritual objects and art.

Out of respect for the sanctity of the Torah, during public
readings the parchment is touched with a surrogate implement, called a
yad (pointer). Traditionally the yad almost always bears a small hand

with index finger extended at the tip. Silversmith Anika Smulovitz created a pair of Torah pointers that address her aspirations to go deeper into the text, in particular the scholarly textual debate over the identification of multiple authors of the Torah. Smulovitz's silver implements *Octogenarian* (2002) and *Compass* (2002) combine scientific tools with the traditional form of the pointer to allow the contemporary user to navigate the complexities of a text recast as a landscape. Like Alix Mikesell, Smulovitz combines the fine metal of silver with mass-produced materials to create unexpected hybrids, where the plastic elements evoke objects external to Jewish ritual. This new sensibility can be compared to the work of modernist Judaica artist Kurt Matzdorf, who began using brightly colored acrylic in his silverwork in the late 1960s as a decorative element to express contemporary taste, not to evoke an extra functionality.

The most festive of Jewish holidays, Purim, involves the raucous reading of a scroll, the Book of Esther. JT Waldman's comix version is sensual and thoughtful, combining fin-de-siècle Secession style with midrash embedded in the text as marginalia and stories within stories. A key innovation of *Megillat Esther* (2005; p. 93) is the resolution of English and Hebrew reading in opposite directions. In the middle of the book, at a critical juncture in the story when King Ahashveros has convulsive dreams presaging the reversal of the Jewish death decree, Waldman requires the reader to flip the book and proceed in the opposite direction, disorienting and making the reader more aware of the physical act of storytelling. Creativity within actual or self-imposed constraints is a contemporary ethic that melds with Jewish ritual.

Artists have used intricate and detailed drawings with Jewish forms to digest the chaos of daily life in many ways. In her ongoing *Alchemy* drawing series, Suzanne Treister mashes up a daily newspaper with ancient alchemical symbols. The headlines and images of fears of global warming on the front page of the London *Independent* of June 28, 2007, are arranged along the *sephirot*, the chart of the ten attributes of God that Kabbalists believe contains the divine plan for the world. Deborah Grant also riffs on hermetic patterns of Jewish thought to seek hidden causalities. Grant's work on the American cult leader David Koresh (né Vernon Howell) is shaped in the Hebrew letter *vav*, assigned the value of six in Jewish numerology, or *gematria*. Grant's piece displays her collage method of "random select" and splits into the absurdity of free association Koresh's

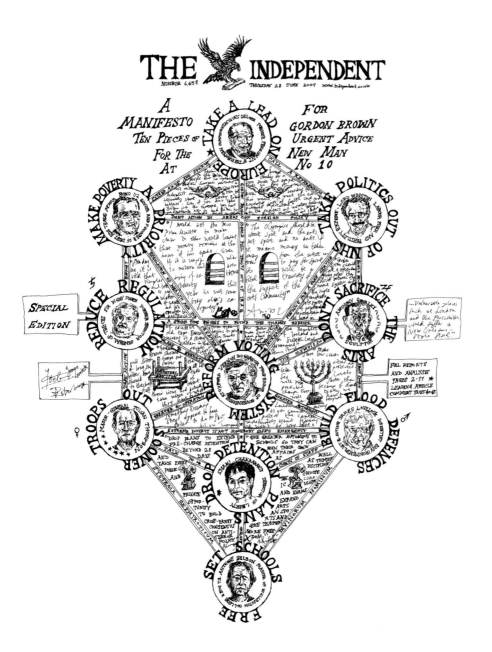

This piece is from a series in which I transcribed front pages of daily newspapers into alchemical drawings, reframing the world as a place animated by strange forces, powers, and belief systems. These works redeploy the languages and intentions of alchemy: the transmutation of materials and essences of the world as a text, as a realm of powers and correspondences that, if properly understood, will allow humans to take on transformative power. In working with this series, I began with a tight conceptual structure and then allowed subconscious and intuitive decisions to take place within it.

— SUZANNE TREISTER

SUZANNE TREISTER
(British, b. 1958)
ALCHEMY/The Independent, 28th June 2007, 2007
Rotring ink on paper, 16 ¾ x 11 ¾ in. (42.6 x 29.9 cm)
Courtesy of Annely Juda Fine Art, London, and P.P.O.W. Gallery, New York

The title (6 + 6 + 6 = 18 & 1 + 8 = 9) & 9 inverted is 6 is a play on the myths and conspiracy theories that are usually attributed to anti-Semitic and racist rants. Although anti-Semitic and racist conspiracy theories have not been accepted in mainstream circles, the myths sometimes creep deep into the popular psyche. The detailed marks of oil paint and archival ink throughout the work are a stream of consciousness mark-making. Unedited spontaneous marks are a way of portraying my viewpoint on the issues through a code I call "Random Select."

— DEBORAH GRANT

DEBORAH GRANT
(American, b. 1968)
*(6 + 6 + 6 = 18 & 1 + 8 = 9) & 9
inverted is 6,* 2008
Oil and archival ink and mixed media
on birch panel, 54 x 30 in.
(137.2 x 76.2 cm)
Courtesy of the artist and Steve Turner
Contemporary, Los Angeles

The seven drawings that comprise Sephirot are a "game piece" that take my ongoing time-based work into an exploration of omer, the seven-week period between Passover and Shavuot. Each week is sequentially represented by a Star of David, containing seven geometric elements. Using events of Jewish concern as a parameter, I created a drawing each day throughout this period. For the duration of the omer I became the proverbial "wandering Jew," and the drawings chronicle my journey. The omer binds the notion of Passover's freedom to Shavuot's practice of ritual. The ritualistic parameters and constraints that I select afford me greater creative freedom.

— MARTIN WILNER

MARTIN WILNER
(American, b. 1959)
Sephirot, 2007
Ink on paper, number 1 of 7 pieces,
each 11 1/4 x 11 1/4 in.
(28.6 x 28.6 cm)
The Jewish Museum, New York, Purchase:
Contemporary Judaica Acquisitions
Committee Fund, 2009-22.1-7

The counting of the omer *represents the relationship between
a person and his or her community. Beginning with one,
we become an ordered multitude—accruing the attributes of
a people in our journey from slavery to redemption. For
decades, I thought about how to embody this paradox in a
work of art. The omer counter that resulted consists of
forty-nine sculpted forms set in a grid; each one can be placed
in its designated space in only one way. By a daily act, the
viewer becomes a participant in the continually changing work,
a celebration that takes place over measured time.*

— TOBI KAHN

TOBI KAHN
(American, b. 1952)
Saphyr, 2002
Acrylic on wood, 27 ½ x 22 ¼ x 9 ½ in.
(69.9 x 56.5 x 24.1 cm)
The Jewish Museum, Purchase: Aryeh
Raquel Rubin/Targum Shlishi
Foundation, Nick Bunzl, Goldman-
Sonnenfeldt Foundation, Mavin I. Haas,
and Daniel and Elizabeth Sawicki, Gifts;
and Contemporary Judaica Acquisitions
Committee Fund, 2004-22a-xx

claim to be the incarnation of ancient Persian emperor Cyrus (in Hebrew, Korush), who allowed the Jews to return from Babylonian exile to the land of Israel. Grant's title, *(6 + 6 + 6 = 18 & 1 + 8 = 9) & 9 inverted is 6* (2008), challenges how conspiracy theorists attach vav to Satan's number of 666, as a means of imposing a pseudostructure of mystical formula on the chaos of daily life.

The act of counting—of measuring days—is a fundamental element in the double consciousness of Jewish thought and its connection to the cycles of nature. One of the most intense periods of counting is the forty-nine-day period between the second night of Passover (the Exodus from Egypt) and the first night of Shavuot (the giving of the law on Mount Sinai), a period beginning with a special offering of the first of the barley harvest at the ancient Temple in a quantity called the *omer*. Martin Wilner's *Sephirot* (2007) consists of seven Stars of David. Each star represents the seven days of the week. Each day of the omer period, Wilner selected an image of a person who is somehow connected to an eclectic Jewish identity, from celebrities in the news to acquaintances. Wilner then drew the image in one corner or the central field of one star. Thin lines link the bodies of the subjects, suggesting an organic structure of the Jewish mind as if produced in a solitaire version of the Dadaist game "exquisite corpse." One of the most engaging interpretations of the counting of the omer is Tobi Kahn's painted wood *Saphyr* (2002). The format is a simple grid, each quadrant representing a single day. To use the object, one must place a peg on the board, reenacting the bringing of the omer to the Temple. By turning thought into interactive sculpture, Kahn has invented a new public practice of counting.[52]

Helène Aylon also renders rituals of Jewish thought into sculptural installation. *All Rise* (2007; p. 80) formalizes her fantasy of a Jewish religious court (*beit din*) run by women to supplant sexism in the traditional adjudication of Jewish ritual. Aylon considers the work to be the concluding installation in a remarkable series of artworks interrogating sexism in Jewish law and ritual, which began with her monumental installation *The Liberation of G–d* (1996). Perhaps we can best trace the evolution and the emergence of a new aesthetic sensibility in comparing the two pieces. The older work gains power from its critical force. Aylon covered each page of the five books of the Bible with vellum. She then meticulously highlighted every line she considered sexist. The visitor flipped through the pages of the book and witnessed the extent to which the founding text of Judaism is rife with misogyny. The piece aestheticizes frustration and anger and posits no easy solution.

In contrast, *All Rise* presents a positive vision of the future: dark-stained wood courtroom furnishings, in the style of typical masculine authority, are flanked by a pair of pink flags, and a pink hyphen appears in the word "G-d." This installation is a dream of a female Jewish court. Although women preside in liberal beit din, they do not yet preside in Orthodox courts nor in any Jewish religious court in Israel, where Orthodoxy is the law of the land. Aylon's work imagines a feminist *halacha* (Jewish law), a fusion of beliefs considered inherently oppositional. In contemporary practice they are steadily finding common ground. Orthodox individuals and institutions in the United States and Israel are starting to allow women to participate at the highest levels, with several granting women *semicha*, or rabbinical ordination, following the decades-long practice in the liberal branches of Judaism. The dialectic between present realities and tradition inspires an ongoing process of reinvention.

The works in *Reinventing Ritual* survey a new aesthetic sensibility of the twenty-first century. The common thread is hybridity achieved through the reinterpretation of the actions of ritual. The approach and style are inclusive of all levels of Jewish knowledge and observance, age, gender, nationality, or religion. The works present Judaism as a lived, vital, heterogeneous, multicultural, contradictory process that is open and malleable. Although this type of Judaism might not be familiar or comfortable to all Jews today, it is the strongest expression of the contemporary aesthetic and values in advanced art, design, craft, and architecture. Artists focus on the action of ritual to develop a fresh, direct contact with the varieties of Judaism and to share the experience with others, like a nice plate of finely chopped noodles.

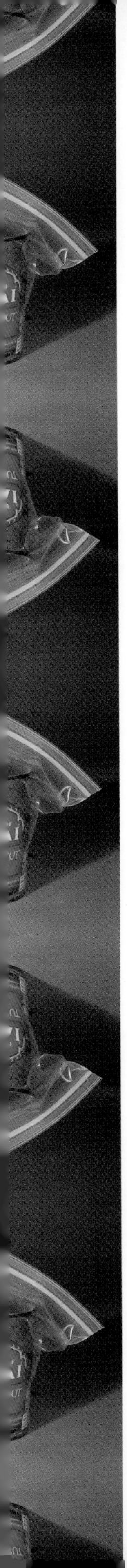

JULIE LASKY

"How Can I Simply Throw Away These Shoes That Have Served Me So Well?"

RECYCLING AND JEWISH RITUAL

WHEN THE JEWISH RECONSTRUCTIONIST CONGREGATION OF EVANSTON, Illinois, set out to build the most environmentally responsible house of worship ever raised in America, it turned to Chicago architect Carol Ross Barney, who reclaimed wood siding from barns in upstate New York, procured high-efficiency glass, and installed a solar-powered eternal light. Green architecture offers efficient ways to acquire and transport materials and to heat and cool interior spaces—activities that demonstrate respect for the earth but also save money. Many progressive organizations today, religious or secular, embrace eco-friendly building strategies. In pursuing the highest standard of sustainable architecture for its new building, a platinum certification from the U.S. Green Building Council's LEED (Leadership in Energy and Environmental Design) program, the JRC in Evanston invoked not just the environment and the economy but also biblical law: the edict of *bal tashchit*.[1]

As written in Deuteronomy 20:19-20, bal tashchit inveighs against the destruction of fruit trees in wartime.[2] Centuries of rabbinical commentary have expanded this tenet into a law against wanton destruction and wasteful behavior; bal tashchit has come to address both the sacred (an order to respect God's handiwork) and practical (advice not to waste any earthly material that can clothe, shelter, or nourish you).[3] By assigning value to the most humble of resources, bal tashchit tosses a democratic

47

The new shul *for the Jewish Reconstructionist Congregation (JRC) is a 31,600-
    square-foot facility replacing an existing 21,400-square-foot synagogue
    on the same site. JRC's commitment to the principle of* tikkun olam *(repairing
    the world) is manifest in the construction of a sustainable and ethical
    architecture. The form and the material of the building, a precious wooden
    box, are a visual testament to these values. The character of the JRC's
    highly involved, multigenerational congregants is reflected in the informal,
    nonhierarchical community and worship spaces. On a modest budget of
    $230 per square foot, the shul has achieved an LEED Platinum certification,
    a primary goal set by the congregation's board of directors.*

— ROSS BARNEY ARCHITECTS

ROSS BARNEY ARCHITECTS
*Jewish Reconstructionist
Congregation,* Evanston,
Illinois, 2008
Courtesy of Ross Barney
Architects, Chicago

cloak of sanctity over a wide swath of creation, natural and manmade, animated and inert. It requires that one distinguish between objects worthy of preservation and those judged to be useless or worse. As written in the Sefer ha-Chinuch, the thirteenth-century Spanish compilation of Jewish law, "The purpose of this *mitzvah* is to teach us to love that which is good and worthwhile and to cling to it, so that good becomes a part of us and we will avoid all that is evil and destructive. This is the way of the righteous and those who improve society, who love peace and rejoice in the good in people and bring them close to Torah: that nothing, not even a grain of mustard, should be lost to the world."[4]

The Jewish Reconstructionist Congregation building is the only work in The Jewish Museum's exhibition *Reinventing Ritual* to refer directly to bal tashchit. And yet its principle of active conservation is at the heart of the exhibition. For it is impossible to convey the significance of any revised ritual without preserving some aspect of the tradition that underlies it, baring the question of essence: How far can one deviate from the gestures, artifacts, and symbols of religious devotion without obscuring meaning? What makes ritual ritual?

Many artists in this exhibition employ recycling as an important strategy for creating ritual objects. The incorporation of old materials into new forms is central not just to the JRC temple, whose foundation was created in part from the demolished building that had occupied its site, but also to Johnathan Hopp and Sarah Auslander's seder plates produced from flea-market dishware, Allan Wexler's charity boxes based on existing food packages, and Barbara Rushkoff's *Plotz* zine, which incorporates vintage drawings from old Hebrew textbooks. More tangentially, recycling is alluded to in the nineteenth-century-style wedding dress designed and hand-sewn by Liora Taragan, Galya Rosenfeld's Torah curtains made of IKEA fabric, Norm Paris's ersatz-rubble and Virgil Marti's skeletal-finger mezuzahs, and Francisca Benitez's video of sukkahs built in Williamsburg, Brooklyn. If the artists do not consciously observe bal tashchit in repurposing materials and ideas from other sources and times, they are united in respecting the law's embrace of the modest and exalted as interdependent components of a single creation.[5] Often, their reinvented objects achieve a higher state of spirituality through personification, animating an inert material by evoking the user engaged in ritual. Marti's mezuzah formed from the fiberglass cast of a finger bone, for instance, anticipates the living

finger that will repeatedly touch it, and Liora Taragan's wedding dress is shaped to suggest the body within.

Just as the JRC building aligns with a global, secular movement to preserve natural resources, this exhibition's subsidiary theme of recycling dovetails with the activities of many contemporary designers. Conscious of the ecological damage and exploitative labor conditions provoked by industrial production, designers throughout the world have embraced recycled and recyclable materials, developing a visual language that signals their social and environmental consciousness. Consumer objects are more likely than ever to look handcrafted with rough textures and neutral palettes, to glorify materials that until recently were considered disposable, such as cardboard and cork, and to rescue and reform consumer castaways, from tires to magazines. It was in this spirit that the Dutch designer Jo Meesters recently created his Pulp series of vases, pitchers, and bowls from a lumpy concoction of paper pulp and polyurethane applied to found vessels (FIG. 1), that the New York-based designer Stephen Burks developed his Love furniture collection for the elite Italian manufacturer Cappellini from the confetti of shredded periodicals (FIG. 2), and that the Parisian designer Thaddée de Slizewicz produced containers hand-sewn from discarded rubber tires for the online modern furniture retailer Design Within Reach (FIG. 3).

Unlike the creations of 1980s postmodernism, an era that also cherished humble materials—consider the experiments with plastic laminate undertaken by Italy's

As designers we approach the world of Judaica
with great interest; we enjoy the complete merging
of the simple explanation and the homiletic
interpretation of every object. The menorah
contains symbols and meanings from the
period of the First Temple. Some interpretations
associate the menorah with the unity of Israel.
Its construction and its very existence as one unit
are illustrative of this unity. We created a
menorah from a solid body with seven floating
single candlesticks from different origins
and periods. The solid body with its clean shape
encloses complexity and diversity.

— REDDISH STUDIO

REDDISH STUDIO:
NAAMA STEINBOCK
(Israeli, b. 1975) and
IDAN FRIEDMAN
(Israeli, b. 1975)
Menorah, 2008
Various metals, steel frame,
11 3/8 x 15 11/16 x 3 1/2 in.
(29 x 40 x 9 cm)
Courtesy of the artists, Sitriya, Israel

Memphis movement—the sustainability imperative results in designs that are singularly lacking in irony. Postmodernism celebrated despised genres for the shock value; it depended on challenging Western culture's faith that wood was superior to plastic, solid superior to veneer, and the Memphis of ancient Egypt superior to the Memphis of Elvis Presley. But today's recyclers, like the artists and designers represented in *Reinventing Ritual,* treat their mongrel productions as opportunities to be inclusive and uplifting rather than to amplify the disparity between high and low.

An important difference is in their treatment of context. Postmodernism, which was fixated on collapsing the plane between past and present, as well as between original and appropriated creative property and between repellent and revered aesthetics, was ultimately object-centered. Today, its iconic productions, such as Ettore Sottsass's vibrantly hued Carlton room divider (1981) and Philip Johnson's AT&T (now Sony) Building with its oversized Chippendale pediment (1978-84), are its best summation. Current designers who are inspired by the principles of sustainability, on the other hand, are more process-oriented. Their works are defined as much by an arc extending from production to use as by the forms they employ—forms that are frequently neutral or seemingly accidental, if not banal. Maxim Velčovský's lopsided *Catastrophe Vase* (2007; FIG. 4), for example, is cast in porcelain, hand-coated with debris, and embedded with the Prague-based designer's own artifacts, such as keys. And yet the lumpy vessel is not meant to challenge one's notion of beauty but is intended to be instantly recognized as beautiful. Whereas postmodernism conspicuously grafted historical references onto contemporary objects, Velčovský's vase is all but timeless (it requires a second look to identify it as a product of the last two millennia). It was made to look eroded. Continuity is its theme, just as continuity, in the form of ritual, connects the objects in this exhibition.

FIG. 4. Maxim Velčovský, *Catastrophe Vase,* 2007. Cast in porcelain, hand-coated with debris, and embedded with artifacts. Courtesy of Qubus Design

For the past few years I have been referencing the tradition of bone chapels in Europe, such as the Capuchin chapels in Rome. And my work has often involved crafting sculptures that could be used in some way, either as furniture or as lighting. Having been raised by a superstitious mother, I tried to follow the required mezuzah protocols faithfully while working with my usual materials and iconography. The idea of touching something every time when entering and leaving a home was something I could relate to.

— VIRGIL MARTI

VIRGIL MARTI
(American, b. 1962)
Untitled (Mezuzah), 2007
Forton MG, fiberglass, epoxy resin, aluminum leaf, plastic parchment, 6 ¼ x 2 ½ x 1 ⅜ in.
(15.9 x 6.4 x 3.5 cm)
Courtesy of the artist, Philadelphia

In the Torah we read "between the lines" with
interpretations. My designs are as much
about the negative space between the
shapes as the positive Magen-David shapes
themselves. I think about the Torah as
a light that illuminates our lives, and the
modular textiles allow light through.
The fabric is reflective so that it increases
the light. Interconnectedness is vital
in Jewish thought and is a big part of the
design of the modules and the way they
work together to create pattern. Pattern
has the power to move us to a meditative
state similar to that of reading prayer.

— GALYA ROSENFELD

GALYA ROSENFELD
(Israeli, b. United States 1977)
Caporet, 2007
Polyester, 18 x 63 in. (45.7 x 160 cm)
Courtesy of the artist, Tel Aviv

Parokhet, 2007
Polyester, 37 x 63 in. (94 x 160 cm)
Courtesy of the artist, Tel Aviv

Recycling in Judaism is as old as the Book of Exodus. In the catalogue for *From the Secular to the Sacred*, a 1985 Israel Museum exhibition of Jewish ritual objects incorporating everyday materials, Iris Fishof identifies biblical and Talmudic examples of recycling, including a laver in the Tabernacle made from mirrors (Exodus 38:8) and an altar plated with metal reused from censers (Numbers 16:39).[6] As Fishof notes, Jewish law prescribes that everyday objects may be reused for spiritual functions but that sacred artifacts cannot be pressed into humble service–"What is holy we must raise [in honor] but not bring down" (Menahoth 99a).[7]

How the recycled artifact is subsumed into the ritual object has been a preoccupation of scholars and rabbis since at least the Middle Ages. According to the Judaica expert Vivian B. Mann, a considerable amount of what we know about medieval fashion is owed to rabbinical cogitation on such questions as placing Islamic prayer rugs next to the Torah ark in a Spanish synagogue or recycling the vestments of Catholic priests acquired by moneylenders into Jewish prayer shawls in Germany.[8] Certainly, a Diaspora people must be resourceful. Objects that survive displacement from homeland to homeland as they're passed down through generations assume the emotional potency of relics. The exhibition catalogue *From the Secular to the Sacred* features, among many other examples, a nineteenth-century German Torah binder made from the cloth on which an infant was circumcised, an eighteenth-century Italian case holding circumcision instruments that evolved from a rococo jewelry box, and an eighteenth-century Austrian Hanukkah lamp created from an embossed brass portion of a soldier's hat.[9] Rather than be preserved in a fragmentary state, such goods as a wedding dress turned into a Torah curtain are knitted into the fabric of ongoing observance, making ritual–the repetitive exercise that unites members of a faith across space and time–into a dynamic practice.

Galya Rosenfeld's Torah curtain (*Parokhet*, 2007) and ark cover (*Caporet*, 2007) exemplify the literal act of weaving together the sacred and humble. These textiles are made from polyester curtains bought at IKEA, the global purveyor of low-cost design, much of it styled in the neutral language of modernism. IKEA's universal aesthetic unites cultures as assuredly as religious ritual seals them off from one another, and Rosenfeld, an Israeli artist and designer, alludes to the tension. Her synthetic material relates to the contemporary democracy of mass-market merchandise (with its poverty of craft), but her intricate pattern, which evokes the Star of David, suggests

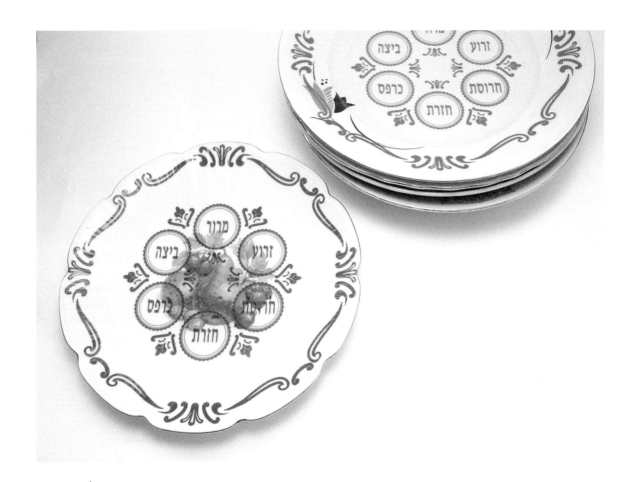

The Passover Plates *are made using old plates we bought at the Jaffa flea market, with an image of a traditional Passover plate fired onto them using a ceramic decal. Firing them in the kiln also burned away any leftover* chametz *and prepared them for Passover. We were interested in the idea of taking discarded, forgotten objects and transforming them into precious objects traditionally seen as heirlooms.*

— JOHNATHAN HOPP AND SARAH AUSLANDER

JOHNATHAN HOPP
(Israeli, b. 1975) and
SARAH AUSLANDER
(Israeli, b. United States 1973)
Passover Plates, 2004-5
Porcelain, ceramic decals,
dimensions variable
Courtesy of the artists, Tel Aviv

Do-It-Yourself Charity Box *was inspired by the traditional charity of canned food drives and by the Pop Art symbol of Andy Warhol's Campbell's Soup can. Although frequently precious and beautifully crafted, anything can be transformed into a tzedakah box. Like the Pop artists, the* Do-It-Yourself Charity Box *offers an experience that opens eyes to the visual symbols of the commercial designs that surround us. These tzedakah boxes are international and cross-cultural. It is when we sit down to eat that we traditionally pause to remember those less fortunate.*

— ALLAN WEXLER

ALLAN WEXLER
(American, b. 1949)
Do-It-Yourself Charity Box, 1999
Canned goods, paper, pen, label, plastic bag, can opener, 7 ½ x 6 ¼ x 2 ½ in.
(19.1 x 15.9 x 6.4 cm)
Courtesy of Ronald Feldman Fine Arts, New York

Gardening Sukkah *unites the Jewish*
harvest celebration and the
activity of gardening. The sukkah
is a ritualistic house erected
at harvest time to celebrate the
bounty and give thanks. For
seven days Gardening Sukkah
shelters the family as they
gather for Sukkot meals. For the
remaining 358 days it functions
as an outbuilding for gardening
activities and storage.

— ALLAN WEXLER

ALLAN WEXLER
(American, b. 1949)
Gardening Sukkah, 2000
Wood, gardening implements,
eating utensils, 108 x 108 x 120 in.
(274.3 x 274.3 x 304.8 cm)
Courtesy of Ronald Feldman Fine
Arts, New York

the particularity of age-old cultural practice.

Like Rosenfeld, the Israeli designers Johnathan Hopp and Sarah Auslander converted humble materials into religious objects, but rather than base their alchemy on the painstaking manipulation of fabric, they exploited the random effects of heat. Their *Passover Plates* (2004-5) are porcelain dishes rescued from flea markets, covered with textual decals signifying the seder's ritual foodstuffs, and fired in a kiln. Hopp and Auslander discovered two advantages in baking the dishware at 1,500 degrees Fahrenheit: they were able to observe the edict of removing any crumb that might contain leavening (a practice usually accomplished through boiling), and they were able to witness unique, unpredictable effects in the glazing. In one instance, Hopp recalled, cracks in an original dish were even repaired.[10]

Passover, Hopp noted, is the most popular holiday in the Jewish calendar, observed by religious and nonreligious families alike. "Everybody celebrates it," he said. "It's not a point of conflict, which is very rare in Judaism and in Israel." The designers' desire to promote inclusiveness extended to the dishware itself. "We wanted to take something discarded, for whatever reason, and elevate it to an heirloom," Hopp said. In transcending its secular origins, this project recalls seder plates repurposed from oyster dishes obtained as souvenirs from central European resorts such as Karlsbad (now in the Czech Republic) in the early twentieth century (FIG. 5).[11] By integrating the dishes into a "family" and promoting them into a caste

FIG. 5. Twentieth-century porcelain seder plate, originally meant for serving oysters, from Karlsbad, Czechoslovakia. Photograph from Iris Fishof, *From the Secular to the Sacred: Everyday Objects in Jewish Ritual Use* (Jerusalem: Israel Museum, 1985), 57

(bottom) FIG. 6. Michelle Ivankovic, *Frosine Glasses*, 2007. Glasses from Goodwill, sandblasted finish. Created for Umbra U+ Studio Collection. Courtesy Umbra

of collectibles, Hopp and Auslander also mirror the secular designs of a number of other contemporary practitioners. Michelle Ivankovic, for instance, used the mismatched offerings of the Goodwill center next to her office in Toronto for her recent Frosine collection of frosted glassware for the household products company Umbra (FIG. 6).

The active, all-embracing quality of ritual is what inspired the New York artist Allan Wexler to produce his *Do-It-Yourself Charity Box* (1999), a modern interpretation of the *tzedakah* cans he recalls from his grandparents' kitchen. Blue and white, like the Israeli flag, the original cans were distributed by charitable organizations. "My grandparents would make a point of cleaning out their pockets and dividing the change between four or five cans on the windowsill," Wexler said.[12] His own charity boxes are bagged assemblages of packaged foods from a variety of cultures, evoking an international "canned good drive, or a soup kitchen. . . . I was interested in the idea of charity crossing borders." A blank label allows users to inscribe the charity of their choice. The food can be distributed in its containers or it can be dished out and the cans reused for collecting donations.

Trained as an architect, Wexler is known for work that blends into design because of its obvious functionality. As in much of his art, Wexler's cans promote active participation. "Charity is one of the greatest of all interactive art forms," he said. The artifacts of ritual are subordinated to the gesture of giving, so that one is left with a shell—a hollow package— that waits to be filled with coins but reaches aesthetic completion only when emptied.

The same process-oriented spirit of renewal can be found in Wexler's *Gardening Sukkah* (2000). Any sukkah, or temporary shelter that houses families during the Jewish harvest holiday, involves material reuse. Rabbi Binyomin Adilman, the former head of a Jerusalem yeshiva, explains that sanctity flows when rituals are transferred to new applications: "For example, the lulav (willows and myrtles that are waved on Sukkot) are put away and later used for fueling the fire that burns the chametz (leavened products) on Erev Pesach. The etrog from Sukkot is poked full of cloves and used to make a fragrant pomander for the Havdalah service at the conclusion of Shabbat. . . . Olive oil from the Land of Israel is hung in the Sukkah as a representative of one of the seven species of the land. It is then saved to use for lighting the Chanukah lights. In addition, a small amount is squeezed out of the wicks, and is eaten six weeks later on Tu B'Shevat."[13]

The video Sukkah *captures the transformation of the Orthodox Jewish neighborhood of Williamsburg, Brooklyn, over the holiday of Sukkot in the year 2000. I was interested in the awakening of this dormant city, latent in a text, built, unbuilt, and rebuilt year after year. I was also interested in the dialogue between the ephemeral city of Sukkot and New York as the host city: how a sukkah occupies a space, adapting itself contextually and inversely; how mutations occur in building typologies to better accommodate Sukkot. I created this video paying close attention to the relation between architecture and performance in this ritual.*

— FRANCISCA BENITEZ

FRANCISCA BENITEZ
(Chilean, b. 1974)
Sukkah, 2001
With music by Memo Dumay, 2006
DVD, sound, 12 min.
Courtesy of the artist, New York

Wexler's *Gardening Sukkah* takes the idea of sustaining a holiday spirit even farther. Outfitted with all the tools needed to produce a crop, his structure is intended for use throughout the year and not merely during the week of Sukkot. At holiday time, the building is transformed from a potting shed into a shelter, replete with dishes and utensils for consuming the harvest. The structure, like Wexler's charity box, embodies a perpetual cycle of renewal, moving between uses without ever lying fallow.

More traditional are the little buildings portrayed in Chilean-born Francisca Benitez's 2001 video *Sukkah*, which are assembled, occupied, and dismantled in typical fashion over the course of a single holiday period. The twist comes from their context: these sukkahs are erected in Williamsburg, Brooklyn, against the stolid faces of tenement buildings—some close to the ground, others suspended on fire escapes, where they seem to cling to the buildings like barnacles clustered on the sides of old ships. Benitez's sukkahs personify their Orthodox makers, who have colonized an environment and whose rituals are enclosed. We see the shelters mostly from the outside—brief occupants of an alien land in a long history of transience.

A house representing an invisible resident also describes Liora Taragan's *Wedding Dress* (2001). "I made it look like it was used, and used a lot," the Israeli artist said, adding, "The idea was to make the garment look like something living was inside."[14] Taragan based her design on Victorian fashion—"the period when the body was not exposed"—and added a "little tallit," the fringed undergarment commonly worn by Orthodox Jewish men. She visually aged the white silk taffeta by steeping it in tea, then dyed parts of the fabric with black ink to combine earthiness with spirituality and conflate marriage and funeral references: "A wedding is death for a young woman," Taragan said. "She's reborn into a world of grownups." As with Velčovský's *Catastrophe Vase*, continuity is the artist's theme, life and spirit flowing into death and matter, with no real demarcation. In the universe of Taragan's dress, recycling is creation. Creation is a throwback. Everything is sustained because nothing really expires.

"There are many ways to look at a fragment; it is both a lost piece from a larger whole and at the same time a new, independent, finite object," the Philadelphia artist Norm Paris wrote in a statement accompanying *Rubble Fragment 1 (Mezuzah)* (2007), a work that, like Taragan's dress, might seem at first sight a desecration rather than a reimagining of ritual.[15] The

63

In this work, the wedding dress is an ultra-Orthodox symbol,
    blurring boundaries and assimilating elements from the
    worlds of the man and the woman in this community.
    The white gown, which symbolizes purity and the sanctity
    of marriage, is stained with the signs of life in the areas
    involved with daily life, such as the hands and feet, whereas
    in the area around the head—the spiritual world—the
    white is dazzling. The use of the symbolism of white and
    black unites life and death, sorrow and joy, spiritual
    and physical, heavenly Jerusalem and earthly Jerusalem.

— LIORA TARAGAN

LIORA TARAGAN
(Israeli, b. 1974)
Wedding Dress, 2001
Taffeta, silk, wire, ink, 63 in. high
(160 cm)
Courtesy of the artist, Tel Aviv

mezuzah appears to be a small rough chunk of concrete torn from a wall, with electrical cable attached, and is meant to invoke the ravages of conflict throughout the Middle East and Jewish history. But that is only one association. The artist has long worked with a material that resembles concrete because it suggests both synthesis and decay: concrete, an aggregate of dust, also eloquently testifies to the forces of entropy, either natural or imposed through aggression. "The dust congeals into a substance that becomes dust itself," he said. In recycling this material, Paris saw a revised perception of myth and allegory: "I am not entirely sure whether this object is a protective talisman, a religious reminder or a symbol of territorial struggle," he wrote.

Paris described his material as at once "prehistoric and post-apocalyptic." The materials Barbara Rushkoff recycled for her *Plotz* zines straddle two distinct periods that are much more closely situated to each other: the mid-twentieth century and the 1990s, when Rushkoff's little magazines appeared. Rushkoff (then Barbara Kligman) began producing *Plotz* in 1995 to "make Judaism cool."[16] Growing up in Philadelphia in the 1960s and 1970s, she was conscious of the dearth of Jews represented in popular culture. She pointed out that even in the 1990s, characters in the sitcom *Seinfeld*, who might variously be described as nebbishes, schnorrers, kibbitzers, and nudges and who socialized on New York's Upper West Side, were never shown to observe Passover.

Among the exhibited works described in this essay, the early issues of *Plotz* are the most postmodern—that is, its recycling ethos is heavily ironic. Rushkoff turned a Jewish lens on everything she encountered and committed irrepressible acts of appropriation. *Plotz*, which like many other zines was produced in small editions on an employer's photocopier, was styled after such publications as the Michelin Guide (containing Rushkoff's account of a trip to Paris), the children's magazine *Highlights*, and *Cliffs Notes*, and featured columns teaching Yiddish vocabulary and identifying famous Jews throughout history, particularly those who tried to hide their heritage. Because Rushkoff lacked artistic training, she used found art for illustration, relying particularly on vintage images of people in old Hebrew textbooks that were sold on New York's Lower East Side. Rushkoff's trademark act of embellishment was to draw Jewish stars on their eyes, a gesture of mixed affection and aggression that left no ambiguity about their identities.

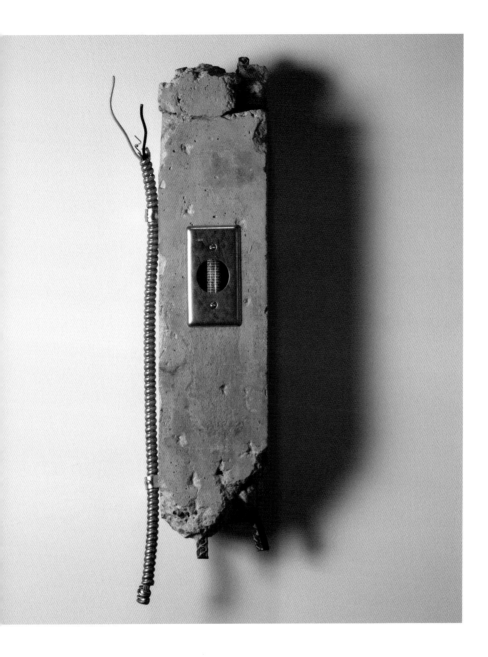

NORM PARIS
(American, b. 1978)
Rubble Fragment 1 (Mezuzah),
2007
Concrete, foam, parchment,
iron, steel, 22 ½ x 6 x 4 ¼ in.
(57.2 x 15.2 x 10.8 cm)
The Jewish Museum, Purchase:
Contemporary Judaica Acquisitions
Committee Fund, 2008-140

Rubble Fragment 1 (Mezuzah) *has been fabricated to look like*
a remnant from a military-industrial site, retrofitted
to become an awkward religious marker. The construct of
Mezuzah is used as a point of departure rather than
as an end in itself. Jewish culture and ritual bridge past
histories and contemporary geopolitics in a conten-
tious web of interrelationships and associations. I am not
entirely sure whether this object is a protective talisman,
a religious reminder, or a symbol of territorial struggle.

— NORM PARIS

Sentinel *and* Embrace *were inspired by my year in Israel*
  (1994–95). In these pieces I explore the intersection of
  opposites—tradition/innovation, facade/interior,
  severity/softness, and found objects/construction. Sentinel
  has a dark, prickly exterior, both menacing and
  defensive. Yet the belly is rubber, suggesting a vulnerable
  side. It references Israel's political position in the region
  and the character of many Israelis I met. Embrace *simultane-*
  ously cradles and deflects. As a Jew I was seduced by
  how comfortable I felt in Israel. But after a year the stress
  and edginess of life there propelled me back to the
  wider opportunities and easy familiarity of the United States.

— ALIX MIKESELL

ALIX MIKESELL
(American, b. 1966)
Embrace, 2003
Silver and plastic reflector,
3 1/16 x 1 5/8 x 1/2 in.
(7.8 x 4.1 x 1.3 cm)
The Jewish Museum, Purchase:
Contemporary Judaica Acquisitions
Committee Fund, 2004-8a–c

BOTTOM
Sentinel, 2003
Silver and rubber, 4 x 1 7/8 x 3/4 in.
(10.2 x 4.8 x 1.9 cm)
The Jewish Museum, Purchase:
Contemporary Judaica Acquisitions
Committee Fund, 2004-7

THE FINAL ISSUE!
#16

$2.00

PLOTZ NOTES

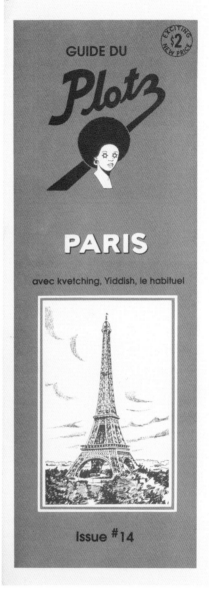

GUIDE DU

Plotz

EXCITING
$2
NEW PRICE

PARIS

avec kvetching, Yiddish, le habituel

Issue #14

Plotz *started out of frustration. When I told a coworker that I didn't want her to decorate my desk at Christmas time with little plastic elves, she looked at me with sheer incredulity. "What DO you do then?" she asked in earnest. Instead of answering her directly, I cranked out the first issue of* Plotz, *which included what Jews do on Christmas, Yiddish sayings, and Jewish members of rock bands. Using clip art in the public domain and inserting Stars of David where I saw fit, I constructed images in* Plotz *that made people look at Jews and Jewishness in a different way.*

— BARBARA RUSHKOFF

BARBARA RUSHKOFF
(American, b. 1961)
Plotz (issue 14), 2001
Printed paper, 11 x 4 in. (27.9 x 10.2 cm)
Plotz (issue 16), 2002
Printed paper, 8 ½ x 5 ⅜ in. (21.6 x 13.7 cm)
Courtesy of the artist, Hastings-on-Hudson, New York

The genuine irony of *Plotz* is that it has itself become a relic. Zine culture went into decline with the birth of the blog, and postmodernism exhausted itself in many forms. Unlike the endlessly iterative act of ritual, postmodernism had a brief, self-consuming life: Where can one go from parody? In 2004, Rushkoff went on to publish a gentle, funny book in *Plotz*'s spirit that purported to demystify the ways of her tribe. Its title: *Jewish Holiday Fun . . . for You!*

In contrast with postmodernism, the impetus for preservation that underlies bal tashchit, as well as a host of twenty-first-century secular designs, involves the primacy of humble substances. Bal tashchit decrees that we sustain a fruit-bearing tree so that it may in turn sustain us. The interdependency is no mocking matter, no opportunity to pit high against low in a contest of spurious values, but a reflection of humankind's role in creation. In a world afflicted by a surplus of carbon dioxide and a dearth of fresh water, many minds are now concentrated on the elemental. Bal tashchit is both a practical gesture of survival and a means of honoring creation's author. Pragmatism and spirituality are entwined in this edict like body and soul.

So it is with recycling, an important sustainable strategy that demands a broad way of understanding objects and the environment. When a material becomes absorbed into a new medium, it challenges definitions of value. What was once whole may now be fragmentary, what was once autonomous may now be integrated, and what was once disposable and rejected may now be an heirloom that can live on forever. Usefulness and adaptability are the keys to transcendence and perhaps even immortality. That is true not just of the artifacts in this exhibition but also of the protean, resourceful Jewish culture that gave rise to them.

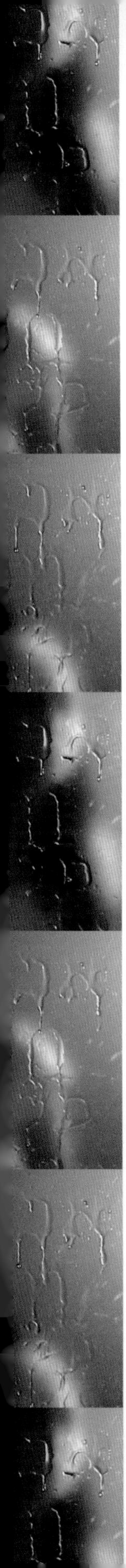

DANYA RUTTENBERG

Heaven
and Earth

SOME NOTES ON NEW JEWISH RITUAL

OVER THE PAST TEN OR SO YEARS, THERE HAS BEEN SOMETHING OF A
cultural explosion as Jews raised on zine culture and riot grrrl came of a
certain age. Jewish-populated urban centers saw a sudden proliferation of
independent prayer groups—the 2.0 version of the 1970s havurah movement.[1] Web sites and blogs catering to folks who lived simultaneously inside
and outside Judaism debuted at an increasingly speedy rate. Magazines
and books by and for the "next generation" of Jews emerged, and hand-screen-
printed T-shirts mashing up Jewish pride and saucy irreverence popped
up everywhere within a short time. Yid-themed literary readings were being
held in hip downtown bars, the Torah inspired graphic novels, and klezmer
became a new kind of punk rock.

   I was twenty-six in 2001 and in the midst of these cultural and
religious offerings emerging from my peers. I began to reconnect with the
part of me that, at sixteen, had loved running around with purple hair
and, at twenty-two, sported sparkly devil's horns. I bought a plain black
yarmulke, and after hot-glue-gunning a gigantic red fake-fur heart to it,
I surrounded the whole thing with rhinestones. I certainly wasn't the only
one out there rocking the Burning Man-goes-to-yeshiva look. *Judaikitsch*,
a guide to blingy ritual craft, came out the very next year, and other folks
I knew were coming up with crazy, unusual, or just unexpected takes
on everything from mezuzah covers to *tzedakah* boxes.[2] One woman even

71

created the outlandish Hanukkah Labia Menorah, a tongue-in-cheek (and, for some, over the line) Jewish expression of sex-positive feminism. These impulses were in effect for a lot of people of my generation—folks felt the desire to situate themselves in Jewish life while embracing a myriad of cultural influences and, maybe, have a little fun at the same time. And in the process, another Jewish aesthetic was born.

But as fresh as our new Jewish models were, in many ways they were just following in the footsteps of those who had come before, both in recent and in preceding generations. That is to say, in some ways the second half of the twentieth century heralded a (counter)-cultural sea change in terms of how Jews do ritual, and in other ways it offered just another take on nothing new under the sun.

FIG. 1. Bill Aron, *Hallel, Great Barrington, Massachusetts,* 1978. Courtesy of the artist

For example, the havurah movement was born out of the tumultuous 1960s and filled with the same revolutionary spirit of grass-roots organizing that drove many young people in America: returning power to the people. Rejecting many aspects of the synagogue model that had been the defining format of American Judaism and taking inspiration from pietistic Jewish fellowships of eras past, the havurahniks asserted that a community, together, could take control of Jewish learning and decide what worship should look like—even without official clergy leadership.[3] Retreats, such as the 1978 gathering of the New York Havurah at which Bill Aron photographed *Hallel*, became one of the better-known ways that communities came together for reflection in nature and lay-led prayer and study (FIG. 1).

The transformation was wrought in decisions large and small—everything from seating arrangements to the content and language of liturgy was questioned, reexamined, and in many cases rebuilt from the bottom up. *The Jewish Catalog: A Do-It-Yourself Kit* was published in 1973, offering a source code to Jews who were spiritually inclined but not yeshiva-trained, in a format that defined a generation (FIGS. 2, 3). *The Jewish Catalog* included instructions for how to tie tzitzit (ritual fringes), how to

One last thing—retreats are really wonderful inventions. Enjoy.

FIG. 2. **Man wearing a tallit climbing tefillin to clouds, from Richard Siegel, Michael Strassfeld, and Sharon Strassfeld, eds.,** *The Jewish Catalog: A Do-It-Yourself Kit* (Philadelphia: Jewish Publication Society of America, 1973). Illustration by Stu Copans. Photograph by Richard Goodbody
FIG. 3. **Drawing from** *The Jewish Catalog*. Illustration by Stu Copans. Photograph by Richard Goodbody

embroider, batik, or tie-dye the prayer shawl on which they would be affixed, how to make kosher wine, how to make mezuzah cases from found objects like walnut shells or toothbrush holders, and, in a classic essay by Arthur Waskow, even how to bring the Messiah.

Around the same time, feminist Judaism emerged, offering a radical vision that sought to transform Jewish life and practice in every way, bringing women and their voices from Judaism's margins into its center. Existing concepts were reworked; for example, Rosh Chodesh, the celebration of the new moon, was rescued from the footnotes of history to become an occasion for women to meet regularly in ritual space, and Passover—the holiday famously marking liberation from oppression—was imbued with feminist symbolism.[4] Early feminists asked questions about who was permitted to perform what rituals and serve in what roles, and they scoured Jewish history and text for role models that had too long been out of the spotlight. With the feverish urgency of people whose very lives were staked on the enterprise, they refashioned existing Jewish rituals and created countless more to consecrate, mark, and make holy many moments in women's lives that had heretofore been ignored—such as the birth of a baby girl, first menstruation, and menopause. They also brought the Jewish sacred into events such as healing from a rape, miscarriage, abortion, or abusive relationship.

Thus the spirit of contemporary Jewish American DIY was born, half a generation before the phrase itself entered the parlance of punk. (In fact, the expression "Do-It-Yourself" came into being as part of the late-nineteenth-century Arts and Crafts movement, in response to the perceived soullessness of industrial culture. It has, perhaps, enjoyed such a long life span precisely because its original raison d'être remains all too relevant today.)

Of course, the 1960s and 1970s were hardly the first time in Jewish history that laypeople took responsibility for their Jewish lives—they have

been engaging in everything from amulet-making to Jewish legal civil dis-
obedience for almost as long as we have texts to tell us anything.[5]
Medieval and early modern Ashkenazi women composed *thkines*, prayers
meant to fill in the spiritual moments ignored by male-authored liturgy.
Supplications for everything from bread-making and childbirth to a safe
return for a spouse traveling abroad filled in the white spaces of women's
lives. And though no one is quite sure about the precise origins of *tashlich*
(casting bread into the water at the New Year as a way of symbolically
casting out one's sins) and *kapparos* (sacrificing a chicken just before Yom
Kippur as a way of effecting atonement), it's clear from rabbinic protests
against both practices that they were created by the people and for the people
and presumably filled a need that was deeper than the desire to obey
local rabbinic authorities. Laypeople have always had an important hand in
the ongoing creation of Judaism.

And of course, innovations of a learned elite are as fundamental a
part of Jewish life as one can find, from the Book of Deuteronomy's central-
ization of cultic rites to Rabbinic Judaism's radical insistence that, in the
absence of a Temple at which to offer animal sacrifice, prayer could serve
as proper worship.[6] More modern examples abound, as well: Kabbalists
invented the Tu BiShvat seder to build a bridge between the Four Worlds of
existence and to hasten redemption (these days, environmentalists use it
as a way of celebrating nature's holiness);[7] the practice of studying all night
on Shavuot to create a state of mind appropriate for receiving the Torah
from Mount Sinai is likewise about five hundred years old, also Kabbalistic;
and the bar mitzvah came into prominence during and after the fourteenth
century to help mark the passage to adulthood in a more formal way than
had been done before.

If it can indeed be said that there is one, the Jewish impulse in
ritual is toward adding, toward finding new ways to fill out the nuances
of our awareness of the Sacred, toward trying to concretize the encounter
with the Divine in as many ways as we can from our messy, complex,
variegated lives. New rituals have always been created, and Jews have always
been willing to go outside known and comfortable forms of Judaism to
make this happen.

It's a testament to how deeply these ideas are ingrained in Jewish
culture that even those who regard themselves as living within the bounds of
Jewish law innovate all the time. For example, a fairly basic survey of sacred

sources has led many to conclude that women may indeed take on certain mitzvot from which they have traditionally been exempted.[8] Women have been wearing *tallitot*—prayer shawls with ritual fringes attached—for a generation and a half, and the variety of styles and colors that one now sees on men and women in many synagogues is a direct result of early feminist determination to shake off the perhaps-too-masculine model of blue stripes on white.

And yet, until recently, few women had taken on the practice of wearing a *tallit katan*, in which those same ritual fringes are attached to an

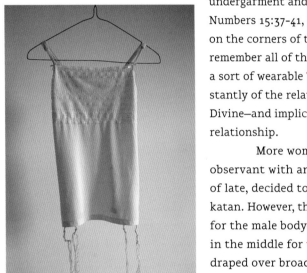

undergarment and worn underneath one's regular clothes. In Numbers 15:37-41, God tells the Israelite people to "put fringes on the corners of their garments…and you will look at it and remember all of the commandments." In other words, tzitzit are a sort of wearable Torah intended to remind the wearer constantly of the relationship he or she strives to have with the Divine—and implicitly to hold him or her responsible to that relationship.

More women of a particular religious orientation—observant with an eye toward egalitarian principles—have, as of late, decided to take on the practice of wearing a tallit katan. However, the garment available in Judaica stores is crafted for the male body—essentially a piece of cloth with a hole in the middle for the head, meant to lie unobtrusively when draped over broad shoulders, a flat chest, a thick waist. It would clearly do so less well over a nonlinear physique, over the same curves given to a woman by her mother and grand-

FIG. 4. Tank-top tzitzit created by Jen Taylor Friedman, HaSoferet.com

mother. Women's clothes don't tend to fit well on top of a lumpy, bulky, ill-fitting garment, and more than one woman I know has worried that her femininity (or femme-ininity) would be compromised by being inscribed in such a "masculine" way.

The solution that many now have found is in a close-fitting tank top, a pack of unattached fringes from a Judaica shop, a pair of scissors, a needle, and some thread (FIG. 4).[9] The stitches on the side of the tank top can be cut open the correct amount to turn it into a four-cornered garment (as it would need to be to be eligible for the fringes). Holes can be cut into each of the four corners and sewed down, and then at each corner the four strings of the fringes can be inserted and tied with the correct series of

75

knots and windings. If one needs it, instructions for tying the fringes themselves can be found in *The Jewish Catalog*. The results are sleek and in accordance with Jewish law.

Several people I know "invented" this model independently; others developed a version of it after hearing of someone else who had used the tank-top modification; word of mouth tends to spread like wildfire, with extra help these days from the Internet. In any case, it's fair to say that the concept of the "female-shaped tallit katan" was born of equal parts old-school feminist entitlement, inspiration from the feminist Third Wave craft resurgence (itself a combination of renewed interest in maligned domestic arts and DIY punkitude), a pinch of help from the havurahniks, and the necessity that engenders invention.

Given the potency and Jewish ubiquity of tzitzit, it's no surprise that *Reinventing Ritual* offers several new takes on the power of the fringe. Rachel Kanter's *Fringed Garment* raises some of the same questions as those of the creators of the tank-top tallit katan, addressing the "feminizing" of what's typically coded as a male garment. However, she offers a very different interpretation, dramatically juxtaposing two seeming extremes—an apron, the ultimate symbol of domesticity and the home sphere with which women in Judaism have been associated; and tzitzit, a positive, time-bound mitzvah, the category of which carries connotations of men's power in the public sphere. Yet Kanter's choice of tzitzit, in this context, is all the more interesting given the particularities of this specific mitzvah. Although it is considered a "positive time-bound mitzvah," from which women are traditionally exempt (but not forbidden), unlike many of the others in this category, it isn't necessarily associated with the public realm. And in fact, even its status as a "positive time-bound mitzvah" was originally more unstable than many of the other mitzvot in this category.[10]

Most striking, Kanter's piece has a textual precedent. The Talmud, in Menachot (43a), tells us, "Rab Judah attached fringes to the aprons of [the women of] his household." This text, which offers a dissenting opinion to the exemption of women to tzitzit, assumed that when women did take them on, they should be attached to their aprons! We see the echo chamber here as a feminist critique of women's traditional roles, a blurring of traditional religious classifications, and an investigation of women's spiritual experience. In some ways this text subverts the usual paradigm of classification, and in other ways it comfortably upholds gender roles and

When I wore a tallit *for the first time, it felt uncomfortable, as if I were wearing my father's overcoat. If I wanted to wear a tallit, it should be made for me. But what would my tallit look like? Using history as a guide, I created a tallit inspired by the four-cornered robes worn by priests in biblical times and designed using vintage apron patterns from the twentieth century. In using traditional sewing techniques I have become part of a long line of women who have created ritual objects using their hands.*

— RACHEL KANTER

RACHEL KANTER
(American, b. 1970)
Fringed Garment, 2005
Cotton fabric, cotton thread, cotton floss, fusible webbing, 42 x 16 in. (106.7 x 40.6 cm)
The Jewish Museum, Purchase: Dr. Joel and Phyllis Gitlin Judaica Acquisitions Fund, 2008-136

Retzuot (ShinShinAgam) *is inspired by the head and arm pieces of tefillin. The straps of tefillin reminded us of electronic conductive wires, which we use in our media-based, audiovisual work. In a similar way, tefillin straps conduct and preserve information that is in the scrolls and that has passed down through history. In* Retzuot (ShinShinAgam), *the scrolls are represented by circuit boards, which generate continuous live video. The video image is a minimal representation of the letter* shin, *which in traditional tefillin appears on the headpiece box.*

— LOVID

LOVID: TALI HINKIS
(American, b. Israel 1974) and
KYLE LAPIDUS
(American, b. 1975)
Retzuot (ShinShinAgam), 2008
Resin, wire, cloth, custom
electronics, video, dimensions
variable
Courtesy of the artists, New York

the patriarchal structure that depicts women as domestic workers and men as legal decision-makers.

Azra Akšamija's *Frontier Vest* uses the same mitzvah to blur the lines of easy categorization even further, offering a portable vest that can be turned into either a tallit or a Muslim prayer rug, thus challenging lines of religious and cultural identification. What would this say about how the wearer embodies himself or herself and about how he or she experiences the act of prayer? Is this an invitation to a universal experience of the Divine, an arrogant disregard for normative religious practice, or both?

Hélène Aylon also refers to tzitzit in *All Rise*, her *beit din* (legal court) for the women throughout history who have not been permitted to serve as religious judges. For *All Rise*, she places tzitzit dangling from the seats of the chairs of the all-powerful judges, presumably women inscribed with a power that traditionally has been in men's hands. Aylon also used tzitzit in another piece not included in this show, creating a provocative *mechitza* (partition between men and women during prayer) out of fringes at the Western Wall, considered by some to be Judaism's holiest site today. For her, the choice of tzitzit in both of these contexts is powerful not only because of their masculine associations but because they are "worn on the groin of males, to combat the lure of women," and thus reflect male sexuality, institutionalized sexism, and patriarchal power.[11]

FIG. 5. Daniel Sieradski, *Tallit Katan Shel Shabbatai Tzvi*, 2005. The artist is pictured at Abu Dis, East Jerusalem. Photograph by Kitra Cahana

Another piece not seen in *Reinventing Ritual* that bears mentioning is the tallit katan crafted by multimedia activist Daniel Sieradski in 2005 (FIG. 5), which, like Akšamija's *Frontier Vest*, asks provocative questions about cultural identity and embodiment. His *Tallit Katan Shel Shabbatai Tzvi*, named for the seventeenth-century false Messiah who eventually converted to Islam, is essentially a standard cloth tallit katan, with tzitzit attached but crafted out of a kaffiyeh, the patterned scarf traditionally worn as a headdress by Arab men and often regarded as a symbol of Palestinian libera-tion. In this piece, then, the volatile terrain of Israeli-Palestinian politics is evoked in a garment aimed to serve the Divine. For Sieradski, this is intentional; he cites classical midrash in which rabbis assert that the Torah seeks to teach us to see all of human-ity as children of Adam, as created in God's image, and to help us to love our neighbor as ourselves.[12] Given that tzitzit are considered the concrete embodiment of the Torah's commandments, Sieradski's goal is to

All Rise *is a* beit din, *a house of law. I petition the traditional beit din of three males to include women as judges. Three elevated chairs are fringed with the tzitzit of religious male garb worn around the groin ostensibly to prevent the lure of women. The conventional sign "In God We Trust" has a pink dash in the word "God," to include the feminine. The flags are pink pillowcases, alluding to my 1980s work when I "rescued" earth in pillowcases. I think of my work as a "rescue" of the Earth and G-d and Women—all stuck in patriarchal designations.*

— HELÈNE AYLON

HELÈNE AYLON
(American, b. 1931)
All Rise: An Installation of a Beit Din as a "House" of Three Women, 2007
Mixed media installation: brass signs, pillowcase flags, chairs, platform, bench, documents, sound, 10 ft., 7 in. x 10 ft. x 5 ft., 5 in. (322.6 x 304.8 x 165.1 cm)
Digital rendering by Stephanie Strogney
Courtesy of the artist, New York

Writing Lesson #1 *is one of a series*
of videos that revolve around a
primal introduction to literacy.
This performance is based on the
Hasidic ceremony in which a
Jewish boy at age three is taken
to school for the first time
and is asked to lick honey off the
Hebrew alphabet so that his
first experience of the language
will be sweet. This work is an
attempt to create a distilled image
of the body as it yearns for
the divine in its initial form—the
alphabet. Re-creating this
ceremony, as a woman and as an
adult, holds a built-in failure
to reach this unattainable divine.
— HADASSA GOLDVICHT

HADASSA GOLDVICHT
(Israeli, b. 1981)
Writing Lesson #1, 2005
DVD, 4 min.
Courtesy of the artist, Jerusalem

force the wearer of his garment to cross even highly contested lines between self and other, to learn to love one's neighbor as oneself—or perhaps the other way around.

Kanter, Akšamija, Aylon, and Sieradski share interests in pushing boundaries and in bringing a host of concerns—feminism, cultural tolerance, the lines between public and private, religious identity—into their investigations of Jewish ritual. And this, too, is par for the course these days. As various movements, issues, and sensibilities have entered Jewish life, they have been able to define and alter its landscape using tools that had already been created, in whole or in part: a Passover "seder in the streets" protests the inequities of the criminal justice system;[13] special penitential prayers for Yom Kippur are crafted to address communal complicity in unjust government policies; the parents of an autistic child craft a ritual of differentiation, modeled after the ritual marking the Sabbath's end, to welcome a child's special needs into the home and community. All these are born out of the notion that Judaism, and Jewish ritual, is a living, constantly growing organism. Abraham Joshua Heschel famously suggested that God's revelation of the Torah is always ongoing; the creators of new ritual and new ritual forms perhaps help us to understand how that Torah might look in the world today.[14]

Why ritual? Why did feminists demand a concrete Jewish marker for processes that have been happening as long as there have been women? Why have gay and lesbian couples been having Jewish commitment ceremonies—huppah, broken glass, and everything—for some time now, even though queer civil unions have only begun to be legal in a handful of states? Why, one might ask, bother at all?

The answer, I think, is this: rituals effect change. They can steer us toward experiences that we might have trouble getting to on our own: take Jewish mourning rituals, for example. We rend our clothing when we hear that a loved one has died, allowing us to externalize anguish and visibly display its aftermath. We stay at home for a week, hiding in a protective cocoon that might help us to deal with our feelings and sense of vulnerability in a way that could be difficult if we were to rush off to work the day after the funeral. During that week, members of the community come by to feed us and offer words of comfort, with the intent of

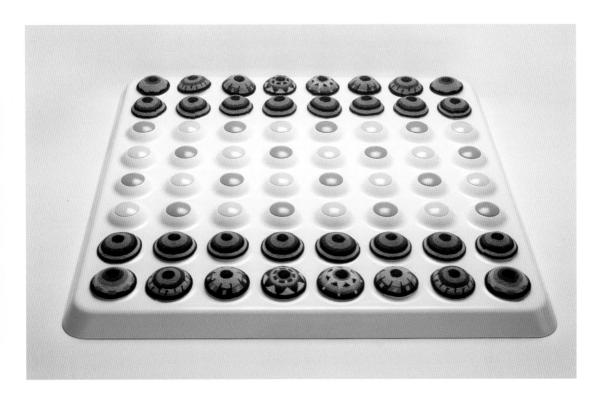

This work stems from the conceptual and
visual analogy between hevruta *learning in*
Beit HaMidrash *and chess competitions.*
In each setting, pairs of contestants (usually
male) sit at a table and confront each
other on the plane of logic until they reach an
arbitration. The skullcaps were handmade
by the female students of the Aviv Yeshiva in
Tel Aviv. Usually, women knit these skull-
caps while studying, traveling by train, or
doing other daily activities. In recent years,
more and more women have had access to
religious colleges that used to be the domain
of male yeshiva students.

— STUDIO ARMADILLO

STUDIO ARMADILLO:
HADAS KRUK
(Israeli, b. 1970) and
ANAT STEIN
(Israeli, b. 1972)
Hevruta-Mituta, 2007
Plastic chess board, thirty-two knitted
skullcaps, 2 3/8 x 27 1/2 x 27 1/2 in.
(6 x 70 x 70 cm)
Courtesy of the artists, Tel Aviv

keeping us from feeling too alone after such a major loss. And traditionally, a mourner goes to synagogue to say the mourner's Kaddish for a
prescribed amount of time.

One can only say the Kaddish among a quorum of Jews, which
forces the person saying it to leave the hermitage of grief. According to most
contemporary customs, mourners stand to recite it—so other people
know immediately who in the room is hurting, who might need some extra
tenderness and care. The prayer itself is a praise of God, said by the
liturgical leader many times in different forms throughout the service, only
a couple of which are designated for grieving. As such, the mourner uses a
prayer that is in some ways a mundane punctuation mark as an expression
of his or her suffering—there's something ordinary and reassuring about
that. At the same time, the words of praise in the prayer force the mourner
to affirm Divine magnificence and glory at the time when things seem
bleakest. A medieval legend suggests that one should say the prayer to help
the soul of the dead in the afterlife, thus giving the mourner one last way
to help connect to the family member he or she has just lost.

Ritual works on multiple planes at once: emotional, physical,
theological, familial, spiritual, social, communal, liturgical. Every rite worth
its salt, every ritual built to last, has at least as many uses and understandings, operates in just as many different ways all at once, and is subject to
just as many interpretations and reinterpretations and renewals of meaning. It's because, I think, there's an indescribable reality underneath the one
for which we have words. Ritual taps into that reality, helps us to work
with it, and employs a network of actions, language, and symbols to effect
what is being signified. If it's ritual done right, it'll work no matter what
explanation we offer for why this might be.

Rituals create change. People come to a ceremony unmarried
and leave married because of the alchemy of blessings and bindings that
happen under the wedding canopy—regardless of what the Supreme
Court of Massachusetts or South Dakota might rule about the legality of
those bindings. Lighting candles transforms ordinary time into sanctified
Sabbath time. Conversion rituals enact the metamorphosis from non-Jew to
Jew, effecting an ontological shift in status. How could we not want to
develop rituals to help us recover from rape or to give us strength as we
begin chemotherapy?

The anthropologist Clifford Geertz once wrote, "In ritual, the world as lived and the world as imagined, fused under the agency of a single set of symbolic forms, turns out to be the same world."[15] In other words, ritual brings the transcendent into our lived experience—or, perhaps more aptly, it opens us up to encounter the One who has been present all along, whether or not we have been experiencing this as such. The symbolic forms enacted in ritual bring earth and heaven together in a way that we are able to see, to understand on some level deeper than rational thought.

For what unites these rituals, new and old, is that they work—that they create an almost indiscernible change in the persons or people undergoing them. They manifest that which cannot ever be articulated in words, and what emerges is never exactly the same as what had begun.

It is not the case that all rituals inscribe themselves directly onto the body, but the body itself is a powerful site for ritual. It makes sense—the use of symbol, gesture, and action to effect change will be especially powerful when impressed directly onto one's physical being. Some of the ways that Judaism does this are obvious, such as the ritual bath in which a woman traditionally transforms herself from a menstruant to one who can return to the marital bed; the fact that baby boys are brought into God's covenant with the Jewish people through *brit milah* (circumcision); and tefillin, the boxes holding special verses worn on the head and arm, affixed with leather straps that literally bind and powerfully heighten awareness during prayer.

But Judaism offers a myriad of ways to bring the full physical self into ritual and worship—the steps and bows that one takes before certain prayers, the gathering of ritual fringes as part of other prayers, the ways in which *havdalah*, the ritual marking the end of Shabbat, engages all of the senses. For, as a ritual marking the differentiation between the holy and the mundane, the person making havdalah tastes wine, smells fragrant spices, sees the shadows created by the flame of a three-wicked candle, hears prayers sung, and holds the ritual objects in hand.

Ritual is, in itself, the embodiment, the enactment, of something that is beyond language and, perhaps, easy comprehension. It's the attempt to bring the transcendent into the world of concrete forms—through words prayed and through manipulation of the material world. Jewish theologian Neil Gillman puts it thusly: "We borrow aspects of familiar human experience to express a complex set of truths about a reality that transcends everyday experience."[16] We use what we have. This is why so many rituals include fire, water, earth, food, wine, or objects worn on the body. This is why so much of video artist Bill Viola's work resonates as deeply religious. Viola uses the four elements to echo the timeless themes of birth and death and rebirth found in many traditions: this is the plane on which human beings operate.

It's probably not a great surprise, then, that much of the ritual innovation of the past thirty or forty years finds the body as its site and that certain groups who have traditionally been disenfranchised from, or pushed to the margins of, Jewish life because of the nature of their bodies would specifically seek out rituals to mark them, celebrate them, or otherwise render

FIG. 6. From *The Mikvah Project*, © 2002 Janice Rubin, mikvahproject.com

them significant. The proliferation of feminist rituals is certainly part of this, as are the many practices now being developed for illness, healing, and disability. One of the most potent sites of recent exploration, however, may be around gender transition, marking the shift from one gender identity into another—often accompanied by very physical changes in the body itself. A number of new rituals have been developed: some use the *mikvah*, the ritual bath, into which a person may be purified and, like a convert to Judaism, reborn (FIG. 6); others adapt baby-naming ceremonies as part of a name and pronoun change or use the model of the bar or bat mitzvah to come into Judaism as a full adult member of one's chosen gender. Micah Bazant chronicled his transition by writing and illustrating *TimTum*, a zine that intersected his body with everything from the Holocaust to the divider separating men and women in prayer (FIG. 7). I know of one transman who recites the Kaddish as he injects the testosterone that helps him grow facial hair, changes his muscular structure, and makes his voice low. He told me that he chose it because the prayer is simultaneously praise of the Divine who has enabled him to do this and also associated with mourning, so that he can ritualize the letting-go of who he once was.

FIG. 7. Micah Bazant, cover of *TimTum* zine.
Courtesy of the artist

And yet, even rituals that seem to mean one thing may mean many things at once. As religion scholar Catherine Bell put it, "The obvious ambiguity or overdetermination of much religious symbolism may even be integral to its efficacy."[17] In other words, rituals are open, and they may even work better when they can mean a lot of things at once. Sometimes we can embrace multiple levels at once, and sometimes we can use the multiplicity of meaning to hear the same radio station on a different frequency.

For example, the biblical prohibition against sexual relations with a menstruant carries a long, misogynist textual history in which women are depicted as filthy and polluting—the dark force that must be controlled. In more recent years, however, some Jewish feminists have argued that the practice surrounding the prohibition is, rather than problematic for women, an opportunity—a way both of honoring the body's natural rhythms and of sanctifying intimate relationships. It can be both of these things, and more, simultaneously and without contradiction.

So when looking at, for example, Tobaron Waxman's *Opshernish*, one may be tempted to read it narrowly. Waxman took his inspiration from the format of the Opshernish (also called Opsherin or Upsherin), a ritual traditionally performed on three-year-old boys on the occasion of their first haircut. In its usual context the ritual is itself an important designator of gender identity. Little boys, up until this point, may have hair that has grown quite long, so apart from sartorial differences, they may be indistinguishable from little girls. The traditional ritual marks the creation of masculinity, for, as these little men emerge from the Opshernish with their newly shorn hair and, perhaps, new *payos* (sidelocks), they also tend to leave the feminine sphere of the mother and may go off to begin Torah study. They become, for the first time, clearly identifiable and socialized as male.

In his piece, Waxman sits in a chair, his long hair tied to the ceiling in locks. Visitors are invited first to snip the hair—leaving each lock suspended and dangling from the ceiling—and then, once his hair is shorn, to assist in shaving his head. Though this piece is complex and multilayered, one might ask whether Waxman appropriated this ritual, in part, as an interrogation of gender's enactment on the body—causing us all to ask what creates gender identity, and how. Was Waxman created male by his haircut? How can ritual change, affect, or trouble our understanding of

Opshernish *is about personal agency, the act of looking, and the eye of the beholder. My* opshern *facilitated an exodus from an infancy of self-awareness and from kinship-based models of identity formation. The hair is both an organic personal document and a social site of expectation. The only way to reclaim my body to myself would be to deconstruct that expectation, by handing the cutting implement to the beholder. Somewhere between embodiment and social construct, both viewer and artist experience a physical change. Tableau vivant captures the moment in which we agree to do this, stretching it out, savoring it, and expanding time.*

— TOBARON WAXMAN

TOBARON WAXMAN
(Canadian, b. 1970)
Opshernish, 2000
Human hair, airplane cable,
mending brackets, barber's
scissors, clippers, razors, two
chrome bowls, shaving cream,
video, sound, installation
dimensions variable
Courtesy of the artist, Toronto

gender? But he also performed this rite as a way of expanding the meaning of the Opshernish's metaphor of growing up and of entering this metaphor on a deeply personal level. He writes, "I suppose that my Opshernish has to do with moving out of a certain infancy of self-awareness and self-conception."[18] And perhaps more radically, Waxman reframes the experience as one that enacts transformation not only on the one whose hair is cut but on all those participating, including those who experience it long after the fact. He writes, "Somewhere between embodiment and social construct both the viewer and the maker/performer experience a physical change."[19] The Opshernish changes all who participate—and perhaps, this is true of the traditional Opshernish as well. As such, Waxman allows us into this ritual's complex layers of meaning in a new and urgent way.

Embodiment happens in many ways. Even Jewish concepts that may seem abstract, like Torah study or God, are brought powerfully into the corporeal. Traditional Jewish texts liken learning Torah to sex, compare the destruction of a Torah scroll to the death of a human being, and speculate on the exact height and dimensions of the Divine, who is beyond human form and measurement.

This notion of encountering Torah in a palpable, physical way is also seen in Johanna Bresnick and Michael Cloud's *From Mouth to Mouth*, which at first blush might seem extremely provocative. In opposition to the religious concern for the preservation and wholeness of sacred books and prohibitions against destroying them, they shredded a Hebrew-English Bible's Book of Leviticus and filled gel capsules with the verses, intended to be swallowed.[20] The artists themselves certainly regard the work as transgressive, describing it as "brazen" and "irreverent."[21] Of course, treating a holy text in this way is outrageous, and their intimations that Torah might be swallowed like Prozac or championed with minimal effort—put in gel caps "for easy consumption"—certainly belie a more Jewishly engaged understanding of how Jews relate to their holy texts.

And yet this notion of internalizing Torah gastronomically is, in its way, traditional. Psalm 34 tells us, "Taste it and you will see that God is good," and the medieval poem "Yedid Nefesh" cries to God to "let Your affection be sweeter than the dripping of a honeycomb or any other taste."[22] In Eastern European towns, children just beginning Torah study would lick honey off tablets on which Hebrew letters were written and receive sweet cakes on which Torah verses were written in order to associate learning with sweetness.

In 2003, dressed as an Orthodox Jewish man (as my alter-ego, Marcus
Fisher), I visited Mount Meron in the north of Israel to take
part in the yearly celebration of Lag b'Omer, commemorating the
death of Rabbi Shimon Bar Yochai. The celebrations are similar
to outdoor raves yet are fueled by religious ecstasy alone. Only men
may dance. Mostly I was terrified that I would be discovered,
outed. Yet the fantasy of being accepted unconditionally into the
tribe, to be accepted as male without being one, to transcend or
mobilize biological limits, or to be embraced purely on the merit
of my intentions and desires kept me going for a few intense hours.
— OREET ASHERY

OREET ASHERY
(British, b. Israel 1966)
Dancing with Men, 2003/2008
Mini DV, color with sound, 5 min.,
22 sec.
Courtesy of the artist, London

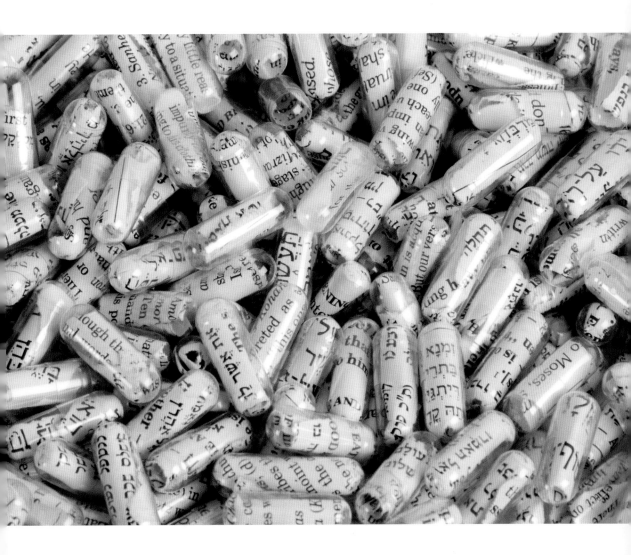

Numerous biblical references speak of the assimilation of spiritual
knowledge through the flesh. It may be transference, as in
Jeremiah 1:9, where God says, "I am putting my words into your
mouth," or it may be "health for the entire body," as is written
in Proverbs 4:20-22. In From Mouth to Mouth we have created
ingestible tablets as a succedaneum for the sacred tablets
they originate from. The text has been dispersed, abstracted,
and diffused into a singular metaphor, to be digested by the
body, mind, and spirit. A transformation has taken place, to be
used as a prescription, a remedy to our questions of identity.

— JOHANNA BRESNICK AND MICHAEL CLOUD

JOHANNA BRESNICK
(American, b. 1973) and
MICHAEL CLOUD
(American, b. 1975)
From Mouth to Mouth, 2006
Bible, gel capsules, installation
dimensions variable
Courtesy of the artists, New Haven
and New York

Perhaps even more resonant with Cloud and Bresnick's work is the Book of Ezekiel, in which God commands Ezekiel to become a prophet and hands him a scroll full of lamentations, presumably reflecting God's sorrow in the face of Israel's rebelliousness. God tells Ezekiel to "eat what you find; eat this scroll, and go and speak to the house of Israel." Ezekiel is said to have "opened my mouth, and He caused me to eat that scroll. And He said to me, son of man, make your belly eat, and fill your bowels with this scroll that I give you. Then I ate it; and it was in my mouth sweet like honey."[23]

The sense, both with Ezekiel and with *From Mouth to Mouth*—as well as, perhaps, the rituals for children starting school—is that learning Torah is about taking it in literally, about letting it become a part of the self and about becoming transformed by the physical and spiritual interaction of the Torah with one's body. Cloud and Bresnick chose verses from the Book of Leviticus, which is simultaneously the Torah's most physical book— dealing, as it does, with sexual prohibitions, animal sacrifice, menstruation, childbirth, and certain kinds of diseases—and its most obscure. The artists describe themselves as "not particularly versed in Judaism," which is telling.[24] Ezekiel ate to internalize God's message and become a prophet. Cloud and Bresnick might have consumed this work to provoke but also perhaps to achieve a sort of union with a text that they may have not felt able to enter in the usual, intellectual way. Perhaps, allowing it to enter them, they may find that they are able to "eat, and be satisfied, and bless."[25]

In some ways, this is the process that we all undergo. For, whether we are consuming them literally or metaphorically, whether we are marked by them in a more concrete or less tangible way, rituals become us, and we become our rituals. They help us to exist in ourselves and in the world in an entirely different way, and therein lies the magic.

The power of *Reinventing Ritual* is that it gives us new ways to encounter, be challenged by, and ultimately be transformed by ritual. This collection of pieces offers fresh understandings of Judaism, Jewish life, and our visions of community, faith, and the Divine. And as such, *Reinventing Ritual* expands our vision of what might be possible in our ongoing attempts to unite heaven and earth.

Most people thought I was crazy for making a comic
  book version of a biblical text. Making the work
  bilingual and requiring the reader to flip the
  book and read in the "opposite" direction was a
  challenging idea. A graphic novel with footnotes and rabbinic citations—how bizarre! Who
  would read such a thing? Would anyone be
  interested in a work embodying the themes and
  ideas of a Jewish holiday practiced for millennia?
  After seven years of research, translation, and
  illustration, I discovered that through repetition
  and focused intention any act or object could be
  ritualized or made holy.

— JT WALDMAN

JT WALDMAN
(American, b. 1976)
Pages from *Megillat Esther*, 2005
Ink on paper, 17 x 22 in. (43.2 x 55.9 cm)
Courtesy of the artist, Philadelphia

TAMAR RUBIN

A Cultural Timeline

1994–2008

1994

FIG. 1. Masada's *Alef* album cover. Produced by Tzadik Records

---

Spertus Institute of Jewish Studies in Chicago establishes Spertus Judaica Prize

Musician and composer John Zorn's *Masada* ensemble releases its first album, *Masada: Alef* (FIG. 1)

Rabbi Menachem Mendel Schneerson, seventh leader of Chabad-Lubavitch, dies at age ninety-two (FIG. 2)

Ma'yan: The Jewish Women's Project holds its first women's seder

Israel and Jordan sign peace treaty

Adam Sandler performs "The Chanukah Song" on *Saturday Night Live*

1995

FIG. 2. "Save the Rebbe's Home" bumper stickers, posters, and buttons (as seen here), were prolific in Hasidic neighborhoods after Rabbi Menachem Mendel Schneerson died. Courtesy of the National Museum of American Jewish History, Philadelphia

---

Writer Jennifer Bleyer self-publishes zine *Mazel-Tov Cocktail*

Writer Barbara Rushkoff publishes first issue of *Plotz* zine (1995–2002)

Yitzhak Rabin is assassinated

YiddishkaytLA is founded to promote Yiddish language and culture

1996   1997

FIG. 3. Cary Leibowitz (American, b. 1963), *Kosher Hot Dog Yarmulke (Please Don't Forget Eleanor Roosevelt), German Yarmulke (Thanks for Remembering), Stonewall Yarmulke (Shalom Independence: June 4, 1776–June 27, 1969), Swedish Yarmulke (Please Don't Forget Raoul Wallenberg)*, 1994–95. Mixed media. Satin, braided trim, metal. The Jewish Museum, New York, Gift of the artist, 1995-97-100

FIG. 4. Cover of Anita Diamant's novel *The Red Tent*

San Francisco-based *Davka* magazine is launched

Photographer Frédéric Brenner publishes *Jews, America*

Sophie Calle's *The Eruv of Jerusalem* photography installation debuts in France

The Knitting Factory club on the Lower East Side of Manhattan hosts the first Downtown Seder

Too Jewish? Challenging Traditional Identities exhibition at The Jewish Museum in New York (FIG. 3)

Jerusalem 3000 International Judaica Design Competition in Jerusalem

First annual Shabbat Across America program

Philip Roth publishes *American Pastoral*, winner of the Pulitzer Prize for fiction

JOFA (Jewish Orthodox Feminist Alliance) is established

Jewish dating Web site JDate is launched

Anita Diamant publishes *The Red Tent*, a novel told in the voice of the biblical character Dinah, daughter of the patriarch Jacob (FIG. 4)

First issue of *Midrasz*, Jewish monthly magazine, is published in Warsaw, Poland

Ma'yan: The Jewish Women's Project and Hebrew Union College mount the exhibition *Drawing from the Source: Miriam, Women's Creativity, and New Ritual*

Tony Kushner's play *A Dybbuk, or Between Two Worlds* opens at the Public Theater in New York (FIG. 5)

South Park episode featuring the song "Lonely Jew on Christmas" airs on Comedy Central

1998   1999

FIG. 5. Tony Kushner's play *A Dybbuk, or Between Two Worlds*, at the Public Theater in New York. Photograph by Michal Daniel

FIG. 6. Marisa Carnesky performing as the Jewess Tattooess in London

Orthodox Union signs a contract with Nabisco, and Oreos become kosher

Sinai Temple launches Friday Night Live, later growing into ATID ("future" in Hebrew), in Los Angeles to serve the young Jewish community

Continuity and Change: Ninety-Two Years of Judaica at Bezalel exhibition in Israel

Madonna acknowledges Kabbalah on her *Ray of Light* album

Israel celebrates its fiftieth anniversary of independence

Israeli-born educator and performance artist Amichai Lau-Lavie founds Storahtelling

Basya Schechter's musical group, Pharaoh's Daughter, releases its debut album, *Daddy's Pockets*

Avoda Arts, a project to integrate the arts and Jewish learning, is launched by Carol Brennglass Spinner and Tobi Kahn

San Francisco-based Be'Chol Lashon is established to address the needs of racially and ethnically diverse Jews

Allegra Goodman publishes *Kaaterskill Falls*, a novel about a 1970s Orthodox summer community in the Catskills in upstate New York

Rabbi Avi Weiss creates modern Orthodox Yeshivat Chovevei Torah Rabbinical School in New York

Marisa Carnesky's live art piece *Jewess Tattooess* debuts in London (FIG. 6)

Kolot: The Center for Jewish Women's and Gender Studies and Ma'yan: The Jewish Women's Project launch Ritualwell, a Web site to inspire innovation in contemporary ritual creation and practice

First issue of *Golem Magazine* is published in Berlin

2000

FIG. 7. Campaign button for presidential candidate Al Gore and running mate Joe Lieberman with their names in Hebrew. Courtesy of the National Museum of American Jewish History, Philadelphia

Birthright Israel sponsors its first free trips to Israel for Jewish young adults

Joshua Venture: A Fellowship for Jewish Social Entrepreneurs is founded in San Francisco (2000-2005)

Ben Stiller, playing a rabbi, and Edward Norton, playing a priest, star in *Keeping the Faith*

First annual European Day of Jewish Culture

Bikkurim: An Incubator for New Jewish Ideas is established

Rabbi Shmuley Boteach publishes *Kosher Sex*

Aldrich Museum in Ridgefield, Connecticut, mounts exhibition *Faith: The Impact of Judeo-Christian Religion on Art at the Millennium*

Al Gore names as his running mate Joseph Lieberman, the first Jewish vice-presidential nominee (FIG. 7)

Second intifada begins in Israel

Five New Yorkers in their twenties launch onlysimchas.com, a Web site for posting news of joyous events, including weddings and births

2001

FIG. 8. **Aerial view of the Jewish Museum Berlin, designed by Daniel Libeskind.** Photograph © Guenter Schneider

Music group Golem is formed, performing klezmer music "with a rock sensibility"

Bet Midrash for artists opens at Schechter Institute in Jerusalem

First class of rabbinical students matriculates at Abraham Geiger College in Potsdam, Germany, the first liberal rabbinical seminary in continental Europe since the Holocaust

Edmund Case founds the independent nonprofit Interfaithfamily.com to encourage the involvement of interfaith families in Jewish life

Adi Foundation, dedicated to exploring the relation between art and Jewish values, is established in Israel

Trembling before G–d, a documentary exploring the lives of observant gay Jews, premieres at the Sundance Film Festival

Shira Chadashah congregation is established in Jerusalem with the goal of providing opportunities for women to lead parts of religious services while adhering to Orthodox *halakha* (Jewish law)

Kehillat Hadar, an independent, egalitarian *minyan* (prayer group), first meets on the Upper West Side of Manhattan

Jewish Museum Berlin, designed by Daniel Libeskind, opens to the public (FIG. 8)

George W. Bush is the first president to hold a Hanukkah candle-lighting ceremony at the White House

2002

FIG. 9. Cover of first issue of *Heeb*

FIG. 10. Melissa Shiff (Canadian, b. 1967), *Elijiah Chair*, 2002. Antique rocking chair, video monitor, and digital video, 33 x 20 x 29 in. (83.8 x 50.8 x 73.7 cm). Used in the Times Square Seder. The Jewish Museum, Purchase: Susan F. Zinder Gift, 2003-26a, b

Brooklyn-based *Heeb* magazine publishes its first issue (FIG. 9)

Reboot, an organization that provides young Jewish adults in North America with opportunities to explore their Jewish identities, is established

Jennifer and Victoria Traig publish *Judaikitsch: Tchotchkes, Schmattes, and Nosherei*, an "inspirational guide to snazzing up tradition"

Ma'yan: The Jewish Women's Project mounts *A Different Purim Sound: Waving Flags and Ringing Bells* at the Manhattan Jewish Community Center, an exhibition featuring flags made by women to be waved when Esther and Vashti's names are read from the Book of Esther on Purim

Artist Melissa Shiff hosts *Times Square Seder Featuring the Matzah Ball Soup Kitchen* on the fourth night of Passover (FIG. 10)

Queer Jews, an anthology, is published

German artist Anna Adam installs the satirical project *Feinkost Adam* at the Jewish Museum of Fürth

JDub Records is started to promote new and innovative Jewish music

2003

FIG. 11. Cover of Jonathan Safran Foer's novel *Everything Is Illuminated*

Inspired by his own experience, Jonathan Safran Foer publishes *Everything Is Illuminated*, a novel about a young Jewish American writer's efforts to research his grandfather's life in Ukraine (FIG. 11)

Sex and the City character Charlotte York, played by Kristin Davis, converts to Judaism and marries fiancé Harry Goldenblatt, played by Evan Handler, in a Jewish wedding

Artist Zoya Cherkassky displays suite of works *Collectio Judaica* in Tel Aviv (FIG. 12)

Synaplex initiative is established by STAR: Synagogue Transformation and Renewal, with the goal of increasing synagogue attendance and building community on Shabbat through innovative programming

Nechama Golan has an exhibition, *A Tent of Her Own*, in Israel

2004

FIG. 12. Zoya Cherkassky (Israeli, b. Kiev, 1976), *Aachen Passover Haggadah*, from the *Collectio Judaica* series, 2004. Screen print on paper, 11 7/8 x 15 3/4 in. (30.2 x 40 cm). The Jewish Museum, Purchase: Phyllis Greenspan Bequest, 2005-31.1

FIG. 13. Cover of Matisyahu's first album, *Shake Off the Dust . . . Arise*, produced by JDub Records. Photograph courtesy of JDub Records

Dara Horn publishes *In the Image*, a novel exploring the significance of faith in the lives of a young Jewish American woman and an older Jewish man who emigrated from Europe

Hebrew College in Boston establishes a transdenominational rabbinical school with Arthur Green as first dean

Pearl Gluck's documentary film *Divan*, an exploration of her Hasidic roots, premieres at Tribeca Film Festival and San Francisco Jewish Film Festival

Nextbook is created to promote Jewish ideas, culture, and literature

Canfei Nesharim organization is established to engage the Orthodox community on environmental issues

Douglas Rushkoff publishes *Nothing Sacred: The Truth about Judaism*

Celebration of 350 years of Jewish life in America

Matisyahu signs with JDub Records and releases first album, *Shake Off the Dust . . . Arise* (FIG. 13)

Rabbi Sharon Brous of Los Angeles founds IKAR ("essence" in Hebrew), a Jewish spiritual community with a focus on social justice

David Katznelson, Amy Tobin, and other San Francisco residents establish DAWN, a contemporary approach to the tradition of all-night study on the holiday of Shavuot

Mayyim Hayyim mikvah and educational center opens in Newton, Massachusetts (FIG. 14)

2005

2006

FIG. 14. Mayyim Hayyim mikvah in Newton, Massachusetts. Photograph © Peter Lewitt 2004

FIG. 15. Stephen Colbert on *The Colbert Report* inviting Jews to call his Atone Phone during Yom Kippur. Courtesy of The Colbert Report

Launch of Jewlicious blog, a forum for different, often irreverent views of Judaism, Israel, and pop culture

Musée d'art et d'histoire du Judaïsme in Paris displays artist Kader Attia's *Big Bang*, a sculpture resembling a meteorite and incorporating the symbols of Judaism (the Jewish star) and Islam (the crescent)

La Petite Jerusalem, a film about a young Orthodox woman attracted to secular philosophy, is released in France

New Holocaust History Museum, designed by Moshe Safdie, opens at Yad Vashem in Jerusalem

Dedication of Holocaust memorial in Berlin, designed by Peter Eisenman

Hekhsher Tzedek initiative is conceived with goal of placing a seal on kosher foods that meet ethical benchmarks, as a supplement to traditional *kashrut* certification

Jewdas, a group dedicated to radical and satirical expressions of Jewish identity, is established in London

JDub Records, Avoda Arts, and the Foundation for Jewish Culture collaborate with the UJA-Federation of New York to create Six Points Fellowships for Emerging Jewish Artists

Kavana, a Jewish cooperative in Seattle, is established with the goal of members drawing from group resources and creating their own Jewish experiences in cooperation with other members

Stephen Colbert features the Atone Phone on Comedy Central's *Colbert Report* (FIG. 15)

Drisha Institute for Jewish Education inaugurates Arts Fellowships Initiative

Ohel Jacob Synagogue, including museum and community center, is dedicated in Munich, Germany, on the sixty-eighth anniversary of Kristallnacht

2007

2008

FIG. 16. Video still from the film *My Mexican Shivah*, directed by **Alejandro Springall**. Cast: Raquel Pankowsky, David Ostrosky, and Emilio Savinni. Photograph by Dante Busquets. © Springall Pictures, Mexico

Morirse está en Hebreo (*My Mexican Shivah*), directed by Alejandro Springall, premieres (FIG. 16)

Mechon Hadar and Synagogue 3000 organizations conduct the National Spiritual Communities Survey

ATARA: The Arts and Torah Association for Religious Artists is founded

First issue of *Jewish Living Magazine* is published

Alexandre Herchkovitch, Brazilian fashion designer, debuts a men's clothing line inspired by traditional Jewish dress

Jewish Theological Seminary announces that it will accept gay applicants to rabbinical and cantorial school

The New Authentics: Artists of the Post-Jewish Generation exhibition opens at Spertus Museum in Chicago

Yad Arts, London, initiates *Other Seder,* with the support of the Jewish Community Center of London, to commission new work from artists of all media that challenges and works with the traditions of the Passover seder

Jewish Reconstructionist Congregation in Evanston, Illinois, dedicates its new platinum LEED-certified green building, the first house of worship in the United States to achieve this certification

The Jewish Museum in New York hosts *Off the Wall: Artists at Work,* an open studio project featuring eleven artists performing and creating art within the Museum

Raid on AgriProcessors kosher meat plant in Postville, Iowa, sparks debate on ethics and kashrut

Great Synagogue in Brussels is rededicated as the Great Synagogue of Europe

Contemporary Jewish Museum in San Francisco opens its new building designed by Daniel Libeskind

Exhibition Checklist

TALILA ABRAHAM
(Israeli, b. 1965)
Dantela, 2004
Stainless steel: etching, 5 x 13 x 13 in.
(12.7 x 33 x 33 cm)
Courtesy of the artist, Kfar Truman, Israel

JONATHAN ADLER
(American, b. 1966)
Utopia Menorah, 2006
High-fired brown stoneware with white
glaze, 9 ⁷/₈ x 11 ¹/₈ in. x 3 ⁵/₁₆
(25.1 x 28.3 x 8.4 cm)
The Jewish Museum, New York, Purchase:
Contemporary Judaica Acquisitions
Committee Fund, 2009-21

CHESELYN AMATO
(American, b. 1958)
Eternal Light, 2003
3M Radiant Light film and wire,
8 x 19 x 7 ⁵/₈ in. (20.3 x 48.3 x 19.4 cm)
The Jewish Museum, New York, Purchase:
Contemporary Judaica Acquisitions
Committee Fund, 2005-33

OREET ASHERY
(British, b. Israel 1966)
Dancing with Men, 2003/2008
Mini DV, color with sound, 5 min., 22 sec.
Courtesy of the artist, London

BRURIA AVIDAN
(Israeli, b. 1966)
Wedding Cup, 2004
Silver, silicone, rubber
3 ⁵/₁₆ x 2 ³/₄ in. (8.5 x 7 cm)
Courtesy of the artist, Har Adar, Israel

HELÈNE AYLON
(American, b. 1931)
*All Rise: An Installation of a Beit Din as a
"House" of Three Women*, 2007
Mixed media installation: brass signs,
pillowcase flags, chairs, platform, bench,
documents, sound, 10 ft., 7 in. x 10 ft.
x 5 ft., 5 in. (322.6 x 304.8 x 165.1 cm)
Courtesy of the artist, New York

SAHAR BATSRY
(Israeli, b. 1974)
Volcano Seder Plate, 2008
Glass, silicone, ½ x 12 in. (1.5 x 32 cm)
Courtesy of the artist, Tel Aviv

FRANCISCA BENITEZ
(Chilean, b. 1974)
Sukkah, 2001
With music by Memo Dumay, 2006
DVD, sound, 12 min.
Courtesy of the artist, New York

MICHAEL BERKOWITZ
(American, b. 1952)
*Fashions for the Millennium: Protective
Amulet Costume*, 2000
Satin: stenciled, jacket: 31 in. long
(78.7 cm), skirt: 38 ½ in. long (97.8 cm)
The Jewish Museum, New York, Purchase:
Dr. Joel and Phyllis Gitlin Judaica
Acquisitions Fund, 2000-75a-h

JOHANNA BRESNICK
(American, b. 1973) and
MICHAEL CLOUD
(American, b. 1975)
From Mouth to Mouth, 2006
Bible, gel capsules, installation
dimensions variable
Courtesy of the artists, New Haven
and New York

ALEXIS CANTER
(American, b. 1981)
Lucky Half, 2004
14K gold, ³/₄ x 1 ¹/₂ in. (1.9 x 3.8 cm)
Courtesy of the artist, Cambridge,
Massachusetts

ALEXIS CANTER
(American, b. 1981)
Wishbone, 2004
14K gold, 1 ¹/₂ x 1 in. (3.8 x 2.5 cm)
Courtesy of the artist, Cambridge,
Massachusetts

ALEXIS CANTER
(American, b. 1981)
Wishbone, 2004
Silver, 1 ¹/₂ x 1 in. (3.8 x 2.5 cm)
Courtesy of the artist, Cambridge,
Massachusetts

AMI DRACH
(Israeli, b. 1963) and
DOV GANCHROW
(Israeli, b. United States 1970)
+/– Hotplate, 2003
Readymade plate, silk-screened
conductive print, abs connector housing,
9 in. diameter (23 cm)
Courtesy of the artists, Tel Aviv

DOV GANCHROW
(Israeli, b. United States 1970) and
ZIVIA
(Israeli, b. 1960)
Netilat Yadayim
(Hand Cleansing Vessel), 2008
Cast ceramic, 15 ³/₄ x 6 in. diameter
(40 x 15 cm)
Courtesy of Loushy Art & Projects, Tel Aviv

HADASSA GOLDVICHT
(Israeli, b. 1981)
Writing Lesson #1, 2005
DVD, 4 min.
Courtesy of the artist, Jerusalem

JOE GRAND
(American, b. 1975)
Galvanized Steel Candelabra, 2003
Steel pipe fittings, 13 x 20 ¹/₂ in.
(33 x 52.1 cm)
Courtesy of Grand Idea Studio, San
Francisco

DEBORAH GRANT
(American, b. 1968)
(6 + 6 + 6 = 18 & 1 + 8 = 9) & 9 inverted is 6,
2008
Oil and archival ink and mixed media on
birch panel, 54 x 30 in. (137.2 x 76.2 cm)
Courtesy of the artist and Steve Turner
Contemporary, Los Angeles

MILA TANYA GRIEBEL
(British, b. 1963)
*"Marriage, I would rather have a cup of
tea!"* 2000
Sterling silver, 1 ⁹/₁₆ x 1 ¹/₄ x ⁹/₁₆ in.
(4 x 3.2 x 1.4 cm)
The Jewish Museum, New York, Purchase:
Contemporary Judaica Acquisitions
Committee Fund and Hyman and Miriam
Silver Fund for Contemporary Judaica,
2008-153

JOHNATHAN HOPP
(Israeli, b. 1975) and
SARAH AUSLANDER
(Israeli, b. United States 1973)
Passover Plates, 2004-5
Twelve plates, porcelain, ceramic decals,
dimensions variable
Courtesy of the artists, Tel Aviv

TOBI KAHN
(American, b. 1952)
Saphyr, 2002
Acrylic on wood, 27 ½ x 22 ¼ x 9 ½ in.
(69.9 x 56.5 x 24.1 cm)
The Jewish Museum, New York, Purchase:
Aryeh Raquel Rubin/Targum Shlishi
Foundation, Nick Bunzl, Goldman-
Sonnenfeldt Foundation, Mavin I. Haas,
and Daniel and Elizabeth Sawicki, Gifts;
and Contemporary Judaica Acquisitions
Committee Fund, 2004-22a-xx

RACHEL KANTER
(American, b. 1970)
Fringed Garment, 2005
Cotton fabric, cotton thread, cotton floss,
fusible webbing, 42 x 16 in. (106.7 x 40.6 cm)
The Jewish Museum, New York, Purchase:
Dr. Joel and Phyllis Gitlin Judaica
Acquisitions Fund, 2008-136

TAMARA KOSTIANOVSKY
(Argentinean, b. Israel 1974)
Unearthed, 2007
Clothing, embroidery thread, metal hooks,
91 x 29 x 33 in. (231.1 x 73.7 x 83.8 cm)
Courtesy of Black and White Gallery,
New York

SIGALIT LANDAU
(Israeli, b. 1969)
Day Done, 2008
With sound work by Yarden Erez
HD-DVD, sound, 17 min., 32 sec.;
9:16 frame
Courtesy of the artist, Tel Aviv

ELAN LEOR
(Israeli, b. United States 1970) and
ERAN LEDERMAN
(Israeli, b. 1970)
Gideon, 2008
Gold-plated brass, blackened
(oxidized) sterling silver, 3 ¾ x ⅝ in.
(9.5 x 1.6 cm)
Courtesy of the artists, Tel Aviv

LOVID: TALI HINKIS
(American, b. Israel 1974) and
KYLE LAPIDUS
(American, b. 1975)
Retzuot (ShinShinAgam), 2008
Resin, wire, cloth, custom electronics,
video, dimensions variable
Courtesy of the artists, New York

VIRGIL MARTI
(American, b. 1962)
Untitled (Mezuzah), 2007
Forton MG, fiberglass, epoxy resin,
aluminum leaf, plastic parchment,
6 ¼ x 2 ½ x 1 ⅜ in. (15.9 x 6.4 x 3.5 cm)
Courtesy of the artist, Philadelphia

MATTHEW McCASLIN
(American, b. 1957)
Being the Light, 2000
Lightbulbs, porcelain light fixtures, metal
electrical conduit, switches, metal
receptacle box, 62 x 44 ¾ x 10 ½ in.
(157.5 x 113.7 x 26.7 cm)
The Jewish Museum, New York, Purchase:
Contemporary Judaica Acquisitions
Committee Fund and Judaica Acquisitions
Fund, 2001-14a-j

MARIT MEISLER
(Israeli, b. 1974)
CeMMent Mezuzah, 2006
Concrete, nickel-plated pewter, 4 ⅝ x 1 ⅜
x ½ in. (11.8 x3.5 x 1.3 cm)
The Jewish Museum, New York, Purchase:
Contemporary Judaica Acquisitions
Committee Fund, 2008-143

ALIX MIKESELL
(American, b. 1966)
Embrace, 2003
Silver and plastic reflector, 3 ¹/₁₆ x 1 ⅝ x ½ in.
(7.8 x 4.1 x 1.3 cm)
The Jewish Museum, New York, Purchase:
Contemporary Judaica Acquisitions
Committee Fund, 2004-8a-c

ALIX MIKESELL
(American, b. 1966)
Sentinel, 2003
Silver and rubber, 4 x 1 ⅞ x ¾ in.
(10.2 x 4.8 x 1.9 cm)
The Jewish Museum, New York, Purchase:
Contemporary Judaica Acquisitions
Committee Fund, 2004-7

RACHEL MOSES
(Israeli, b. France 1963)
Electric Blue/Shocking Pink, from *Dairy
and Meat Dishes*, 2004/2008
Two plates, 10 ½ in. diameter (26.7 cm)
Pencil and watercolor transfer on
porcelain plates
Courtesy of the artist, Paris

RACHEL MOSES
(Israeli, b. France 1963)
Milk/Meat Couples, from *Dairy and Meat
Dishes*, 2004/2008
Two plates, 10 ½ in. diameter (26.7 cm)
Pencil and watercolor transfer on
porcelain plates
Courtesy of the artist, Paris

NORM PARIS
(American, b. 1978)
Rubble Fragment 1 (Mezuzah), 2007
Concrete, foam, parchment, iron, steel,
22 ½ x 6 x 4 ¼ in. (57.2 x 15.2 x 10.8 cm)
The Jewish Museum, New York, Purchase:
Contemporary Judaica Acquisitions
Committee Fund, 2008-140

KARIM RASHID
(American, b. Egypt 1960)
Menorahmorph, 2004
Silicone, stainless steel, 3 ¼ x 11 x 8 ⅛ in.
(8.3 x 27.9 x 20.6 cm)
Jewish Museum Centennial Commission;
Purchase: Tobe Pascher Workshop
Commission Program Fund, 2004-48

REDDISH STUDIO: NAAMA STEINBOCK
(Israeli, b. 1975) and
IDAN FRIEDMAN
(Israeli, b. 1975)
Menorah, 2008
Various metals, steel frame, 11 ⅜ x 15 ¹¹/₁₆ x
3 ½ in. (29 x 40 x 9 cm)
Courtesy of the artists, Sitriya, Israel

TRACY ROLLING
(American, b. 1972)
Ketubah for Tali and Kyle, 2001
Linoleum print, painting, and silk-screen
on paper, 14 x 22 in. (35.6 x 55.9 cm)
Courtesy of Tali Hinkis and Kyle Lapidus,
New York

GALYA ROSENFELD
(Israeli, b. United States 1977)
Caporet, 2007
Polyester, 18 x 63 in. (45.7 x 160 cm)
Courtesy of the artist, Tel Aviv

GALYA ROSENFELD
(Israeli, b. United States 1977)
Parokhet, 2007
Polyester, 37 x 63 in. (94 x 160 cm)
Courtesy of the artist, Tel Aviv

ROSS BARNEY ARCHITECTS
Jewish Reconstructionist Congregation,
Evanston, Illinois, 2008
Architectural model and digital photo-
graphs, installation dimensions variable
Courtesy of Ross Barney Architects, Chicago

BARBARA RUSHKOFF
(American, b. 1961)
Plotz (issue 12), 2000
Printed paper, 8 ½ x 5 ⅜ in. (21.6 x 13.7 cm)
Plotz (issue 13), 2000
Printed paper, 8 ½ x 5 ⅜ in. (21.6 x 13.7 cm)
Plotz (issue 14), 2001
Printed paper, 11 x 4 in. (27.9 x 10.2 cm)
Plotz (issue 16), 2002
Printed paper, 8 ½ x 5 ⅜ in. (21.6 x 13.7 cm)
Courtesy of the artist, Hastings-on-
Hudson, New York

ANIKA SMULOVITZ
(American, b. 1974)
Compass, 2002
Sterling silver, compass, acrylic,
6 ½ x ⅝ x ⅝ in. (16.5 x 12.7 x 12.7 cm)
The Jewish Museum, New York, Purchase:
Contemporary Judaica Acquisitions
Committee Fund, 2008-142

ANIKA SMULOVITZ
(American, b. 1974)
Octogenarian, 2002
Sterling silver, magnifying glass, 7 ⅞ x
¹⁵/₁₆ x ⅝ in. (17.8 x 2.4 x 1.6 cm)
The Jewish Museum, New York, Purchase:
Contemporary Judaica Acquisitions
Committee Fund, 2008-141

STUDIO ARMADILLO: HADAS KRUK
(Israeli, b. 1970) and
ANAT STEIN
(Israeli, b. 1972)
Hevruta-Mituta, 2007
Plastic chess board, thirty-two knitted
skullcaps, 2 ⅜ x 27 ½ x 27 ½ in. (6 x 70 x 70 cm)
Courtesy of the artists, Tel Aviv

STUDIO ARMADILLO: HADAS KRUK
(Israeli, b. 1970) and
ANAT STEIN
(Israeli, b. 1972)
Seder Plate, 2005
Wood, acrylic, 15 ¾ x 18 ½ in. (40 x 47 cm)
Courtesy of the artists, Tel Aviv

LIORA TARAGAN
(Israeli, b. 1974)
Wedding Dress, 2001
Taffeta, silk, wire, ink, 63 in. high (160 cm)
Courtesy of the artist, Tel Aviv

EZRI TARAZI
(Israeli, b. 1962)
Shamno Natan, 2001, produced 2006
Aluminum: anodized and machined; silver
electroplated brass, 2 ⁷/₁₆ x 10 ³/₁₆ x 2 ⁷/₁₆ in.
(6.2 x 25.9 x 6.2 cm)
The Jewish Museum, New York, Purchase:
Contemporary Judaica Acquisitions
Committee Fund, 2007-18

ADAM TIHANY
(Israeli, b. Transylvania 1948)
Mezuzah, 2004
Silver plate: cast, 5 ¼ x 1 in. (13.3 x 2.5 cm)
The Jewish Museum, New York, Jewish
Museum Centennial Commission; Gift of
Christofle, 2004-44

SUZANNE TREISTER
(British, b. 1958)
*ALCHEMY/The Independent, 28th June
2007*, 2007
Rotring ink on paper, 16 ¾ x 11 ¾ in.
(42.6 x 29.9 cm)
Courtesy of Annely Juda Fine Art, London,
and P.P.O.W. Gallery, New York

MIERLE LADERMAN UKELES
(American, b. 1939) and
STEVEN N. HANDEL
(American, b. 1945)
*"I'm Talking to You": A Scent Garden: Three
Different Voices from Nature, Version II*, 2009
Numbered scientific vessels of various
sizes, including petri dishes, beakers,
Erlenmeyer flasks, specimen dishes,
cylinders, and volumetric flasks, and
containing spices, fruits, leaves, roots,
grasses, fragrant oils, seeds, flowers,
herbs, and photographs; mirrored glass
base, acrylic texts, list, diagram, and key,
15 ¾ x 24 x 24 in. (40 x 61 x 61 cm)
Commissioned by The Jewish Museum,
New York

VIGNELLI DESIGNS: LELLA VIGNELLI
(American, b. Italy 1934)
Kiddush Cup, 2007
Silver: hand-worked, height: 5 ½ in.
(14 cm), diameter: 3 ³⁄₁₆ in. (8.1 cm)
The Jewish Museum, New York, Purchase:
Contemporary Judaica Acquisitions
Committee and Tobe Pascher Workshop
Funds, 2008-35

VIGNELLI DESIGNS: LELLA VIGNELLI
(American, b. Italy 1934)
Pair of Candlesticks, 2007
Silver: hand-worked, each: 9 ⅞ x 3 ³⁄₁₆ in.
(25.1 x 8.1 cm)
The Jewish Museum, New York, Purchase:
Contemporary Judaica Acquisitions
Committee and Tobe Pascher Workshop
Funds, 2008-34a, b

JT WALDMAN
(American, b. 1976)
Pages from *Megillat Esther*, 2005
Ink on paper, five pages, four are 17 x 11 in.
(43.2 x 27.9 cm), one is 17 x 22 in.
(43.2 x 55.9 cm)
Courtesy of the artist, Philadelphia

TOBARON WAXMAN
(Canadian, b. 1970)
Opshernish, 2000
Human hair, airplane cable, mending
brackets, barber's scissors, clippers, razors,
two chrome bowls, shaving cream, video,
sound, installation dimensions variable
Courtesy of the artist, Toronto

ALLAN WEXLER
(American, b. 1949)
Do-It-Yourself Charity Box, 1999
Canned goods, paper, pen, label, plastic
bag, can opener, 7 ½ x 6 ¼ x 2 ½ in.
(19.1 x 15.9 x 6.4 cm)
Courtesy of Ronald Feldman Fine Arts,
New York

ALLAN WEXLER
(American, b. 1949)
Gardening Sukkah, 2000
Wood, gardening implements, eating
utensils, 108 x 108 x 120 in.
(274.3 x 274.3 x 304.8 cm)
Courtesy of Ronald Feldman Fine Arts,
New York

MARTIN WILNER
(American, b. 1959)
Sephirot, 2007
Ink on paper, seven pieces, each 11 ¼ x 11 ¼
in. (28.6 x 28.6 cm)
The Jewish Museum, New York, Purchase:
Contemporary Judaica Acquisitions
Committee Fund, 2009-22.1-7

Notes

DANIEL BELASCO "**Chopping Noodles**"

1. Harold Rosenberg, "Is There a Jewish Art?" *Commentary* 42 (July 1966); reprinted in *Discovering the Present: Three Decades in Art, Culture, and Politics* (Chicago: University of Chicago Press, 1973), 223-31.

2. Rosenberg, "Is There a Jewish Art?" 228-29. Thanks to Norman L. Kleeblatt for bringing this aspect of Rosenberg's important article to my attention.

3. Even in the 1990s, Rosenberg's interest in folk arts was not yet validated. See Margaret Olin, "C[lement] Hardesh [Greenberg] and Company: Formal Criticism and Jewish Identity," in Norman L. Kleeblatt, ed., *Too Jewish? Challenging Traditional Identities* (New York: The Jewish Museum, 1996), 39.

4. Harold Rosenberg, "A Parable of Painting," in *The Tradition of the New* (New York: Horizon, 1959), 20.

5. Richard Siegel, Michael Strassfeld, and Sharon Strassfeld, eds., *The Jewish Catalog: A Do-It-Yourself Kit* (Philadelphia: Jewish Publication Society of America, 1973), 40.

6. Barbara G. Myerhoff, "We Don't Wrap Herring in a Printed Page: Fusion, Fictions and Continuity in Secular Ritual," in *Secular Ritual*, ed. Sally Falk Moore and Barbara G. Myerhoff (Assen, Netherlands: Van Gorcum, 1977), 199.

7. Vanessa L. Ochs, *Inventing Jewish Ritual* (Philadelphia: Jewish Publication Society, 2007).

8. For examples, see Charles S. Liebman, "Ritual, Ceremony, and the Reconstruction of Judaism in the United States," in *Art and Its Uses: The Visual Image and Modern Jewish Society*, ed. Ezra Mendelsohn (New York: Oxford University Press, 1990), 272-83; and Samuel Heilman, "Jews and Judaica: Who Owns and Buys What?" in *Patience and Flexibility: Anthropological Perspectives on the American Jewish Experience*, ed. Walter Zenner (New York: State University of New York Press, 1988).

9. Nicolas Bourriaud, *Relational Aesthetics*, trans. Simon Pleasance and Fronza Woods (Paris: Les Presses du réel, 2002), 28-29.

10. There were earlier avant-garde movements in art that employ the forms of Jewish ritual, most notably early twentieth-century Russia, such as El Lissitzky's illustration of the Passover song "Chad Gadya" (1919) and Ignaty Nivinsky's designs for the theater production of *The Golem* (1925). Tom Sandqvist has also detected influences of absurdist Yiddish theater and Hasidic song in the poetry and performance of Romanian-born Jewish Dadaists Tristan Tzara, Arthur Segal, and Marcel Janco. See Sandqvist, *Dada East: The Romanians of Cabaret Voltaire* (Cambridge, Mass.: MIT Press, 2006).

11. Allen Ginsberg, *Howl and Other Poems* (San Francisco: City Lights, 1956), 12.

12. The standard text on the subject is Avram Kampf, *Contemporary Synagogue Art: Developments in the United States, 1945-1965* (Philadelphia: Jewish Publication Society, 1966). For a study of patronage, see Janay Jadine

Wong, "Synagogue Art of the 1950s: A New Context for Abstraction," *Art Journal* 53, no. 4 (1994): 37-43. Modernist music entered synagogues before modernist visual art in the United States. The Park Avenue Synagogue in New York and Congregation Emanu-El in San Francisco commissioned new music by progressive composers Kurt Weill and Darius Milhaud in the 1940s.

13. Marjorie Perloff, *Poetic License: Essays on Modernist and Postmodernist Lyric* (Evanston, Ill.: Northwestern University Press, 1990), 228.

14. Richard Cándida Smith, *Utopia and Dissent: Art, Poetry, and Politics in California* (Berkeley: University of California Press, 1995), 221.

15. Rebecca Solnit, *Secret Exhibition: Six California Artists of the Cold War Era* (San Francisco: City Lights Books, 1990), 21.

16. For a critique of the lack of seriousness in Berman's work, see Matthew Baigell, *American Artists, Jewish Images* (Syracuse, N.Y.: Syracuse University Press, 2006).

17. Allan Kaprow, "A Statement," in *Happenings: An Illustrated Anthology,* ed. Michael Kirby (New York: Dutton, 1965), 48.

18. Kaprow, "Statement."

19. Ann Temkin, "Barnett Newman on Exhibition," in *Barnett Newman,* ed. Temkin (Philadelphia: Philadelphia Museum of Art, 2002), 64.

20. Allan Kaprow, "Participation Performance," in *Essays on the Blurring of Art and Life,* ed. Jeff Kelley (Berkeley: University of California Press, 1993), 185.

21. Allen Ginsberg, *The Letters of Allen Ginsberg,* ed. Bill Morgan (New York: Da Capo, 2008), 140.

22. Rabbi Louis Frishman, Cantor Mimi Frishman, and Freide Gorewitz generously shared memories of this event with me. I consulted a photocopy of the synagogue's file on the Happening.

23. "John Cage Holds a Jewish Happening," *New York Times,* July 24, 1967.

24. Judith Plaskow, *Standing Again at Sinai: Judaism from a Feminist Perspective* (New York: Harper and Row, 1990), 230-31.

25. For an overview of these developments in academic thought, see Barbara Kirshenblatt-Gimblett, "The Corporeal Turn," *Jewish Quarterly Review* 95, no. 3 (2005): 447-61. See also Howard Eilberg-Schwartz, ed., *The People of the Body: Jews and Judaism from an Embodied Perspective* (Albany: State University of New York Press, 1992).

26. Harriet P. Gross, "Q & A Jonathan Sarna," *Dallas Morning News,* August 16, 2008.

27. Arnold M. Eisen, *Rethinking Modern Judaism: Ritual, Commandment, Community* (Chicago: University of Chicago Press), 257.

28. Niles Goldstein, *Gonzo Judaism: A Bold Path for an Ancient Faith* (New York: St. Martin's, 2006), 90.

29. Douglas Rushkoff, *Nothing Sacred: The Truth about Judaism* (New York: Crown, 2003), 218.

30. The term was popularized in art in the exhibition *Freestyle,* held at the Studio Museum in Harlem in 2001. The Jewish version appeared in 2007 in *The New Authentics: Artists of the Post-Jewish Generation,* the inaugural exhibition at the new building of the Spertus Institute in Chicago.

31. See also Ilil Alexande's documentary *Keep Not Silent: Ortho-Dykes* (2004).

32. The legal scholar Kenji Yoshino uses this term to talk about the effacing of cultural difference in the public arena, recognizing that the process of covering mediates a true self and the outside world. Kenji Yoshino, *Covering: The Hidden Assault on Our Civil Rights* (New York: Random House, 2006).

33. Among the many publications on feminism and Judaism, a good recent survey is Elyse Goldstein, ed., *New Jewish Feminism: Probing the Past, Forging the Future* (Woodstock, Vt.: Jewish Lights, 2008).

34. Rabbi Judith Abrams, for example, wears tefillin made with cotton as opposed to leather straps to bring ethical treatment of animals into daily prayer. Thanks to Rabbi Laurie Phillips for bringing this example to my attention.

35. The Hazon Food Conference in 2007 featured a demonstration of the kosher slaughter of three goats. See Samantha M. Shapiro, "The Kosher Wars," *New York Times Magazine,* October 9, 2008.

36. Other decorated plates in the collection of The Jewish Museum that challenge the ritual function with images and texts of violence and anti-Semitism are an apple-and-honey dish by Helène Aylon (2004) and a seder plate by Zoya Cherkassky (2002).

37. Michael Pollan, *The Botany of Desire: A Plant's-Eye View of the World* (New York: Random House, 2002), xv.

38. The most influential compendia of new and feminist marriage rituals include Rachel Adler, *Engendering Judaism: An Inclusive Theology and Ethics* (Philadelphia: Jewish Publication Society, 1998); and Anita Diamant, *The New Jewish Wedding* (New York: Simon and Schuster, 2001).

39. Anna Chave, *Mark Rothko: Subjects in Abstraction* (New Haven and London: Yale University Press, 1989), 104.

40. Abraham Joshua Heschel, *The Sabbath: Its Meaning for Modern Man* (New York: Farrar, Straus and Young, 1951), 8.

41. Jennifer Cousineau, "Rabbinic Urbanism in London: Rituals and the Material Culture of the Sabbath," *Jewish Social Studies* 11 (Spring-Summer 2005): 36-57.

42. Mitch Ginsberg, "How Green Was My City?" *Jerusalem Report,* March 5, 2007, 11. I thank Sigalit Landau for alerting me to this poem.

43. Kathryn Morton, *Judaica Artisans Today: Contemporary Judaica in the United States and Those Who Created It* (Gaithersburg, Md.: Flower Valley Press, 1999), 57.

44. Temple Beth Shalom in San Francisco, designed by Stanley Saitowitz, takes the menorah as structural and symbolic form.

45. Quoted in Jennifer Steinhauer, "Pottery, from Couture to Ready-to-Wear to Mass Market," *New York Times*, August 9, 1998. For greater exploration of these connections, see Matthew Singer's exhibition brochure, "Jonathan Adler, Re: Form" (Philadelphia: Philadelphia Museum of Jewish Art, 2004).

46. Iris Fishof, *From the Secular to the Sacred: Everyday Objects in Jewish Ritual Use,* exh. cat. (Jerusalem: Israel Museum, 1985). I am grateful to Galya Rosenfeld for informing me about this book and its influence on her Torah curtains. See Julie Lasky's essay in this volume.

47. Repurposing, or "Material Redemptionism," is considered a key element of contemporary Israeli design. See Ellen Lupton and Ezri Tarazi, *New Design from Israel* (New York: Cooper-Hewitt National Design Museum, 2006).

48. Rosenberg, "Is There a Jewish Art?" 230.

49. Daniel Boyarin, *Carnal Israel: Reading Sex in Talmudic Culture* (Berkeley: University of California Press, 1993), 5.

50. He also gets his first haircut, in a ceremony called an *upshernish,* the subject of a work by artist Tobaron Waxman, which is discussed in Danya Ruttenberg's essay in this volume.

51. Golan's piece, *Untitled* (2003), appears on the cover of the anthology *Jews and Shoes,* ed. Edna Nahshon (Oxford: Berg, 2008). Also see Judith Margolis, "A Challenging Grittiness: Spirituality in Jewish Women's Art," *Nashim: A Journal of Jewish Women's Studies and Gender Issues* 9, no. 1 (2005): 170-83; and Chava Pinchas-Cohen, "What Is Jewish Expression in Art and Design?" in *Jewish Expression in the Visual Arts?* (Jerusalem: Adi Foundation, 2007), 55-58.

52. Emily D. Bilski et al., *Objects of the Spirit: Ritual and the Art of Tobi Kahn* (New York: Hudson Hills, 2004).

JULIE LASKY "**How Can I Simply Throw Away These Shoes That Have Served Me So Well?**"

1. Author interview with Carol Ross Barney, October 9, 2008. The Jewish Reconstructionist Congregation's Web site provides ample information about the building's sustainable design features as well as a visual tour. See http://www.jrc-evanston.org/. The LEED Green Building Rating System for both new construction and the renovation of exiting buildings has been used to encourage the adoption of sustainable building practices since 1998. Platinum is the highest rating, followed by gold, silver, and certified. Congregation Beth David in San Luis Obispo, California, was the first LEED-certified synagogue. It has a lower rating and a less innovative design than the JRC in Evanston.

2. "When thou shalt besiege a city a long time, in making war against it to take it, thou shalt not destroy the trees thereof by wielding an axe against them; for thou mayest eat of them, but thou shalt not cut them down; for is the tree of the field man, that it should be besieged of thee? Only the trees of which thou knowest that they are not trees for food, them thou mayest destroy and cut down, that thou mayest build bulwarks against the city that maketh war with thee, until it fall." *The Holy Scriptures According to the Masoretic Text*, 2 vols. (Philadelphia: Jewish Publication Society of America, 1955), 1:471.

3. For an analysis of the evolving interpretation of *bal tashchit*, see David Nir, "A Critical Examination of the Jewish Environmental Law of *Bal Tashchit*, 'Do Not Destroy,'" *Georgetown International Environmental Law Review* 18, no. 2 (2006).

4. Quoted on the Web site of the Coalition on the Environment and Jewish Life, http://www.coejl.org/index.php.

5. *Bal tashchit*'s tenet of respecting inanimate matter extends to substances as rudimentary as dust. Rabbi Binyomin Adilman, former head of the Nishmas Chayim Yeshiva in Jerusalem, notes that Aaron instigated two of the ten biblical plagues so that Moses would not be forced to dishonor elements that had protected him. The plague of blood began with the striking of water, a substance that gave Moses sanctuary as an infant, and the plague of lice began with the striking of sand, the material that covered the body of the abusive Egyptian overseer whom Moses killed. "Moses had, so to speak, a debt of gratitude toward the dust and the water, a consideration that applies even to the realm of the inanimate," Adilman wrote. Such tenderness has exerted a powerful influence on Jewish thought, he went on, as in the case of the distinguished Hasidic leader Rebbe Menachem Mendel of Kotzk (1787-1859): "Whenever he [Mendel] replaced a pair of shoes, he would carefully wrap the old worn-out pair in newspaper and only afterwards dispose of them saying, 'How can I simply throw away these shoes that have served me so well?'" Binyomin Adilman, "Recycling in Jewish Tradition," http://www.jewishvirtuallibrary.org/jsource/Judaism/recycling.html.

6. Iris Fishof, *From the Secular to the Sacred: Everyday Objects in Jewish Ritual Use,* exh. cat. (Jerusalem: Israel Museum, 1985), 7.

7. Fishof, *From the Secular to the Sacred,* 8.

8. Vivian B. Mann, ed., *Jewish Texts on the Visual Arts* (New York: Cambridge University Press, 2000), 37-68.

9. Fishof, *From the Secular to the Sacred,* 12, 15, 58.

10. Author interview with Johnathan Hopp, October 20, 2008.

11. For an analysis of this particular example of a recycled ritual artifact, see Felicitas Heimann-Jelinek, "A Plate Crosses Over," in *Position Papers in Preparation for the International Symposium on Jewish Expression in the Visual Arts, February 25, 2007, Jerusalem* (Jerusalem: Israel Museum and Adi Foundation, 2007), 38-42.

12. Author interview with Allan Wexler, October 10, 2008.

13. Adilman, "Recycling in Jewish Tradition."

14. Author interview with Liora Taragan, October 11, 2008.

15. Author interview with Norman Paris, October 13, 2008.

16. Author interview with Barbara Rushkoff, October 14, 2008.

DANYA RUTTENBERG **"Heaven and Earth"**

1. See below for an explanation and description of the havurah movement. In brief, it is a movement that originated in the late 1960s and early 1970s of lay Jews who organized themselves for community and worship.

2. Jennifer Traig and Victoria Traig, *Judaikitch: Tchotchkes, Schmattes, and Nosherei* (San Francisco: Chronicle, 2002).

3. *Havurah* means fellowship, coming from the word *haver,* or friend.

4. For example, a "Miriam's cup" full of water was placed on the table as a feminist parallel to the Elijah's cup of wine; an orange was placed on the seder plate to symbolize the empowerment or inclusion of marginalized Jews (there are several stories about the orange's original intended meaning); feminist *haggadot* were written using creative rituals and alternatives to male-centered language and practices; and all-women seders began to take place, sometimes in addition to, and sometimes in place of, a traditional (and/or mixed-gender) seder.

5. A few examples: the daughters of Israel, it says in the Talmud (Niddah 66a), took extra stringencies upon themselves in the observance of laws surrounding menstruation, to the detriment of their husbands' sexual access to them, and these measures became codified; later, Maimonides complained that Egyptian Jewish women who did not like these same stringencies—at that point considered a requirement—had simply stopped observing them. Similarly, the idea

that wigs might be a suitable form of head-covering for married women in the Jewish world is said to have evolved in sixteenth-century France and Italy, where Jewish women, following local fashions, insisted on wearing them (instead of headscarves of some sort) over the protests of rabbinic authorities. Eventually the rabbis, loath to declare them all sinners, permitted the practice.

6. It should be noted that this substitution of prayer for sacrifice actually originated in the Book of Deuteronomy—if the aforementioned cultic rites were to take place only in Jerusalem, those without easy access to the Temple would need some way to communicate with God; as such, the Torah for the first time commands the recitation of liturgy (e.g., 21:8-9, 26:1-11, and 26:12-15). This tendency intensified during the Babylonian exile after the destruction of the First Temple, but even so, the ability of the post-Second Temple rabbis to create an entire religion out of a Judaism that had heretofore revolved almost entirely around the Temple cult and its sacrifices was nothing short of extraordinary.

7. Some streams of Kabbalistic thought describe four worlds of existence, each closer to the Divine from the material world or further from it. They are called, respectively, the worlds of action, formation, creation, and, closest of all to the Godhead, emanation.

8. Mishnah Kiddushin 1:7; Tosefta Kiddushin 1:10; Babylonian Talmud (BT) Eruvin 96a and Rosh Hashonah 33a; the stam in Sifrei Bamidbar 115; the Tosafot commentary on BT Kiddushin 31a (regarding BT Baba Kama 87a); the Tosafot commentary on BT Brachot 14a; Maimonides *Mishneh Torah Hilchot Tzitzit* 3:9; Rabbi Nisim ben Reuven (the Ran), commentary on Rabbi Isaac ben Jacob Alfasi (the Rif) Rosh Hashonah 955; Rabbi Moses Isserles (the Rema), commentary on the *Shulchan Aruch Hilchot Tzitzit* Orech Hyim 17:2; Rabbi Moses Isserles (the Rema), commentary on the *Shulchan Aruch Hilchot Tzitzit* Orech Hyim 589:6; Rabbi Moshe Feinstein, *Iggerot Moshe* Orech Hyim 4:49; Rabbi Eliezer Yehuda Waldenberg, *Tzitz Eliezer* 9:2; as well as the opinions of Rashi, Rebbeinu Tam, Rashba, and others.

9. For more precise instructions, and a few more notes on how to do this in accordance with Jewish law that are not included here, please go to http://danyaruttenberg.net/2005/04/05/diy-mitzvah-gear/.

10. See the Tosefta Kiddushin 1:10 and BT Menachot 43a. I would argue that the fact that the rabbis even have to explain why tzitzit are a positive time-bound mitzvah (coupled with Rab Judah's dissenting opinion about its status mentioned in this essay) testifies to the fact that its categorization was not originally clear. For more on women and positive time-bound mitzvot, see http://danyaruttenberg.net/2004/11/22/i-am-positive-that-my-time-is-bound-by-mitzvot/.

11. Author correspondence with Daniel Belasco, February 17, 2008.

12. Sifra Kedoshim 4:12.

13. See Jo Hirschmann and Elizabeth Wilson, "Next Year in Freedom! Taking Our Seder to the Streets," in *Queer Jews*, ed. David Schneer and Caryn Aviv (New York: Routledge, 2002), 258-69.

14. See, e.g., Abraham Joshua Heschel, *Heavenly Torah: As Refracted through the Generations*, trans. Gordon Tucker and Leonard Levin (New York: Continuum, 2005).

15. Catherine Bell, *Ritual Theory, Ritual Practice* (New York: Oxford University Press, 1992), 27.

16. Neil Gillman, *Sacred Fragments: Recovering Theology for the Modern Jew* (Philadelphia: Jewish Publication Society, 1990), 81.

17. Bell, *Ritual Theory, Ritual Practice*, 184.

18. Tobaron Waxman, "Opshernish," *GLQ: A Journal of Lesbian and Gay Studies* 7, no. 4 (2001): 681-87.

19. Waxman, "Opshernish."

20. See, e.g., Deuteronomy 12:3-4 and Rashi on Deuteronomy 12:4, Rambam *Hilchot Yesodi HaTorah*, chap. 6, esp. 6:8, and in the Babylonian Talmud, Shavuot 35a, Shabbat 115a-b, Eruvin 98a-b, as well as the Yerushalmi Eruvin 10:3.

21. Correspondence between the artists and Daniel Belasco, and Belasco's notes from a subsequent telephone conversation with Johanna Bresnick, August 30, 2007.

22. Psalm 34:8.

23. Ezekiel 3:1-3.

24. Notes from Daniel Belasco's telephone conversation with Johanna Bresnick, August 30, 2007.

25. Deuteronomy 8:10.

117

Bibliography

Adi Foundation. *Borders of Sanctity in Society, Jewish Thought, and Art.* Exh. cat. Jerusalem: Keter, 2003.

———. *Light in Literature, Art, and Jewish Thought.* Jerusalem: Adi Foundation and Am Oved, 2005.

———. *Midrash: Jewish Expression in the Visual Art.* Jerusalem: Adi Foundation, 2007.

Baigell, Matthew. "Spiritualism and Mysticism in Recent Jewish American Art," *Ars Judaica* 2 (2006): 135-51.

Boris, Staci. *The New Authentics: Artists of the Post-Jewish Generation.* Exh. cat. Chicago: Spertus Museum, 2007.

Braunstein, Susan L. *Five Centuries of Hanukkah Lamps from The Jewish Museum: A Catalogue Raisonné.* New York: The Jewish Museum; New Haven and London: Yale University Press, 2005.

Calle, Sophie. *L'erouv de Jerusalem.* Arles: Actes Sud, 1996.

Carmon, Efrat, and Nancy Benovitz, trans. *In the Light of the Menorah: Story of a Symbol.* Exh. cat. Jerusalem: Israel Museum, 1999.

Cohen, Julie-Marthe, and Emile Schrijver, eds. *Presenting Jewish Ceremonial Art.* Amsterdam: Menasseh ben Israel Institute for Jewish and Cultural Studies and Joods Historisch Museum, 2001.

Cohen, Julie-Marthe, Jelka Kröger, and Emile Schrijver. *Gifts from the Heart: Ceremonial Objects from the Jewish Historical Museum.* Amsterdam: Joods Historisch Museum, 2004.

Contemporary Jewish Museum. *New Work/Old Story: Eighty Artists at the Passover Table.* Exh. cat. San Francisco: Contemporary Jewish Museum, 2009.

———. *Scents of Purpose: Artists Interpret the Spice Box, April 4–September 5, 2005.* Exh. cat. The Jewish Museum San Francisco, 2005.

Cousineau, Jennifer. "Rabbinic Urbanism in London: Rituals and the Material Culture of the Sabbath." *Jewish Social Studies* 11, no. 3 (2005): 36-57.

———. "The Urban Practice of Jewish Space." In Louis P. Nelson, ed., *American Sanctuary: Understanding Sacred Spaces,* 65-86. Bloomington Indiana: Indiana University Press, 2006.

Dundes, Alan. *The Shabbat Elevator and Other Sabbath Subterfuges: An Unorthodox Essay on Circumventing Custom and Jewish Character.* Lanham, Md.: Rowman and Littlefield, 2002.

Fonrobert, Charlotte Elisheva. "The Political Symbolism of the Eruv." *Jewish Social Studies: History, Culture, and Society* 11, no. 3 (2005): 9-35.

Fonrobert, Charlotte Elisheva, and Vered Shemtov. "Introduction: Jewish Conceptions and Practices of Space." *Jewish Social Studies: History, Culture, and Society* 11, no. 3 (2005): 1-8.

Gliksberg, Naftaly. *Concealed and Revealed.* Exh. cat. Jerusalem: Schechter Institute for Jewish Studies, 2002.

Gomberg, Betsy, and Susan Schaalman Youdovin, eds. *The Hanukkah Menorah: Philip and Sylvia Spertus Judaica Prize.* Chicago: Spertus Museum, 1994.

——. *The Havdalah Spice Container: Philip and Sylvia Spertus Judaica Prize.* Chicago: Spertus Museum, 1998.

——. *Judging the Book by Its Cover: Torah Coverings.* Chicago: Spertus Museum, 2000.

——. *The Seder Plate: The 1996 Philip and Sylvia Spertus Judaica Prize.* Chicago: Spertus Museum, 1996.

Gorlin, Alexander. "Kabbalah and Architecture." *Faith and Form Magazine* 41, no. 2 (2009).

Grafman, Rafi. *Crowning Glory: Silver Torah Ornaments of The Jewish Museum.* Ed. Vivian B. Mann. New York: The Jewish Museum; Boston: David R. Godine, 1996.

Gruber, Ruth Ellen. *Virtually Jewish: Reinventing Jewish Culture in Europe.* Berkeley: University of California Press, 2002.

Gruber, Samuel. *American Synagogues: A Century of Architecture and Jewish Community.* New York: Rizzoli, 2003.

Gruber, Samuel, Michael Levin, and James E. Young, eds. *Jewish Identity in Contemporary Architecture.* New York: Prestel, 2004.

Hartray, John F., and Olga Weiss, eds. *The Chicago Booth Festival: Architects Build Shelters for Sukkot, October 18, 1994–July 26, 1995.* Exh. cat. Chicago: Spertus Museum, 1994.

Hebrew Union College, Jewish Institute of Religion. *Living in the Moment: Contemporary Artists Celebrate Jewish Time.* Exh. cat. New York: Hebrew Union College; Cincinnati: Jewish Institute of Religion, 2000.

Hoffberg, Judith A. *Women of the Book: Jewish Artists, Jewish Themes.* Boca Raton, Fla.: Atlantic University, 2001.

Israel Museum. *The Divine Image: Depicting God in Jewish and Israeli Art.* Exh. cat. Jerusalem: Israel Museum, 2006.

The Jewish Museum San Francisco. *L'Chaim! A Kiddush Cup Invitational*. Exh. cat. San Francisco: The Contemporary Jewish Museum San Francisco, 1997.

———. *Light Interpretations: A Hanukkah Menorah Invitational*. Exh. cat. San Francisco: The Jewish Museum San Francisco, 1995.

———. *Making Change: One Hundred Artists Interpret the Tzedakah Box, November 14, 1999–January 23, 2000*. Exh. cat. San Francisco: The Jewish Museum San Francisco, 1999.

Judisches Museum der Stadt Wien. *Chanukkah*. Exh. cat. Vienna: Judisches Museum der Stadt Wien, 1994.

Kirshenblatt-Gimblett, Barbara, and Jonathan Carp, eds. *The Art of Being Jewish in Modern Times*. Philadelphia: University of Pennsylvania Press, 2008.

Kleeblatt, Norman L., ed. *Too Jewish? Challenging Traditional Identities*. New York: The Jewish Museum; New Brunswick, N.J.: Rutgers University Press, 1996.

Lefkowitz, Lori, and Rona Shapiro. "The Politics and Aesthetics of Jewish Women's Spirituality." *Nashim* 9 (2005): 218-24.

Lipis, Miriam. "A Hybrid Place of Belonging: Constructing and Siting the Sukkah." In Julia Brauch, Anna Lipphardt, and Alexandra Nocke, eds., *Jewish Topographies: Visions of Space, Traditions of Place*, 27-42. Aldershot, England: Ashgate, 2008.

Kaplan, Louis, Andrea Most, and Anna Shternshis. *Command J: Jewish Laws, Digital Arts*. Exh. cat. Toronto: University of Toronto, 2005.

Loewy, Hanno, and Michael Wuliger. *Shlock Shop: Die wunderbare Welt des jüdischen Kitschs*. Berlin: Jüdisches Museum Hohenems Berlin and Mosse-Verlag by Jüdische Presse, 2005.

Magnus, Shulamit. "Reinventing Miriam's Well: Feminist Jewish Ceremonials." In Jack Wertheimer, ed., *The Uses of Tradition: Jewish Continuity in the Modern Era*, 331-48. New York: Jewish Theological Seminary of America, 1992.

Margolis, Judith. "A Challenging Grittiness: Spirituality in Jewish Women's Art." *Nashim: A Journal of Jewish Women's Studies and Gender Issues* 9 (Spring 2005): 170-83.

———. "The Painted Word: Jewish Women's Book Art." *Nashim: A Journal of Jewish Women's Studies and Gender Issues* 8 (Fall 2004): 251-67.

Ma'yan: The Jewish Women's Project. *Miriam's Cups, Drawing from the Source: Miriam, Women's Creativity, and New Ritual*. New York: Petrie Great Hall and the Hebrew Union College Skirball Museum, 1997.

Meitner, Erika. "The Mezuzah: American Judaism and Constructions of Domestic Sacred Space." In Louis P. Nelson, ed., *American Sanctuary: Understanding Sacred Spaces*, 182-201. Bloomington: Indiana University Press, 2006.

Morton, Kathryn. *Judaic Artisans Today: Contemporary Judaica in the United States and Those Who Created It*. Gaithersburg, Md.: Flower Valley Press, 1999.

Ochs, Vanessa. "The Homemade Passover Haggadah." In Colleen McDannell, ed., *Religions of the United States in Practice*, 2 vols. 2:53-66. Princeton: Princeton University Press, 2001.

——. *Inventing Jewish Ritual*. Philadelphia: Jewish Publication Society of America, 2007.

——. "Women and Ritual Artifacts." In Phyllis Chesler and Rivka Haut, eds., *Women of the Wall: Claiming Sacred Ground at Judaism's Holy Site*, 310-34. Woodstock, Vt.: Jewish Lights, 2003.

Ofrat, Gideon. *Thou Shalt Make . . . : The Resurgence of Judaism in Israeli Art*. Exh. cat. Tel Aviv: Time for Art, 2003.

Orenstein, Gloria Feman. "Torah Study, Feminism and Spiritual Quest in the Work of Five American Jewish Women Artists." *Nashim: A Journal of Jewish Women's Studies and Gender Issues* 14 (Fall 2007): 97-130.

Rosenbaum, Belle. *Upon Thy Doorposts: The Law, the Lore, the Love of Mezuzot: A Personal Collection*. New York: Jacob and Belle Rosenbaum Foundation, 1994.

Roth, Laurence. "Oppositional Culture and the 'New Jew' Brand: From *Plotz* to *Heeb* to *Lost Tribe*." *Shofar: An Interdisciplinary Journal of Jewish Studies* 25, no. 4 (2007): 99-123.

Rothschild, Sylvia, and Sybil Sheridan, eds. *Taking Up the Timbrel: The Challenge of Creating Ritual for Jewish Women Today*. London: SCM, 2000.

Rushkoff, Barbara. *Jewish Holiday Fun . . . for You!* New York: Universe, 2003.

Sachs, Angeli, Edward van Voolen, and Samuel Gruber, eds. *Jewish Identity in Contemporary Architecture*. Munich: Prestel, 2004.

Schlossman, Jenni L. "Visual Arts as a Pathway to Prayer and Meditation." In Leonard J. Greenspoon and Ronald A. Simkins, eds., *Studies in Jewish Civilization, Volume 13: Spiritual Dimensions of Judaism*. Omaha: Creighton University Press, 2003.

Siegel, Richard, ed. *On the Future of Jewish Culture in America: Preliminary Findings and Observations*. New York: National Foundation for Jewish Culture, 2002.

Society of American Silversmiths. *Artisans in Silver: Judaica Today*. Exh. cat. Cranston, R.I.: Society of American Silversmiths, 1997.

Soltes, Ori Z. *Jewish Artists: On the Edge*. Santa Fe, N.Mex.: S. Asher, 2001.

Sperber, David. *Between Israel and the Nation: The Relations between Judaism and Islam as Reflected in Local Contemporary Art*. Ramat Gan: Bar-Ilan University Press, 2007.

——. *Broken Vessels: Deconstructive Aspects in Contemporary Jewish Art*. Ramat Gan: Bar-Ilan University Press, 2008.

——. *These Are Your God, O Israel: Light and the Sun as the Iconographic Representation of God in Jewish and Israeli Art*. Ramat Gan: Bar-Ilan University Press, 2006.

———. *Vice Versa: The Culture of the Beit Midrash and Contemporary Jewish Art.* Ramat Gan: Bar-Ilan University Press, 2008.

Stolow, Jeremy. "Holy Pleather: Materializing Authority in Contemporary Orthodox Jewish Publishing." *Material Religion: The Journal of Objects, Art and Belief* 3, no. 3 (2007): 314-35.

Stolzman, Henry, and Daniel Stolzman. *Synagogue Architecture in America: Faith, Spirit, and Identity.* Mulgrave, Victoria, Aus.: Images, 2004.

Traig, Jennifer, and Victoria Traig. *Judaikitsch: Tchotchkes, Schmattes, and Nosherei.* San Francisco: Chronicle, 2002.

Weissbach, Lee Shai. "The Architecture of the Bimah in American Synagogues: Framing the Ritual." *American Jewish History* 91, no. 1 (2003): 29-51.

Weissler, Chava. "'Art Is Spirituality!': Practice, Play, and Experiential Learning in the Jewish Renewal Movement." *Material Religion: Material Cultures in American Jewry* 3, no. 3 (2007): 354-79.

Yeshiva University Museum. *Continuity and Change: Ninety-Two Years of Judaica at Bezalel.* Exh. cat. New York: Yeshiva University Museum, 2000.

Contributors

DANIEL BELASCO is Henry J. Leir Assistant Curator at The Jewish Museum, where he organized the exhibitions *Otiyot: Life of the Letters* and *Art, Image, and Warhol Connections* (with Joanna Montoya). He is co-curator of SITE Santa Fe's Eighth International Biennial (with Sarah Lewis) in 2010. Before arriving at the Museum he was a staff writer for the *Jewish Week* in New York, and he has contributed essays and reviews to *Art in America, ArtNews,* and other journals. He received a Ph.D. in the history of art from the Institute of Fine Arts, New York University, in 2008.

JULIE LASKY is editor of Change Observer, an online magazine about design and social impact. Prior to that she was editor-in-chief of *I.D.*, the magazine of international design. She is the author of two books: *Borrowed Design: Use and Abuse of Historical Form* (1993), written with Steven Heller, and *Some People Can't Surf: The Graphic Design of Art Chantry* (2001). Honors include a National Arts Journalism Program Fellowship at the Medill School of Journalism at Northwestern University and the Richard J. Margolis award for writings on the cultural life of postwar Sarajevo. She recently joined the MFA design criticism faculty at New York's School of Visual Arts.

TAMAR RUBIN was, from 2006 to 2008, Curatorial Program Associate at The Jewish Museum, where she worked with the Judaica collection, assisted with the exhibition *The Dead Sea Scrolls: Mysteries of the Ancient World* (2008), and was curator of *Repairing the World: Contemporary Ritual Art* (2007). She received her B.A. in history from Yale University in 2006 and now lives and teaches in Chicago.

RABBI DANYA RUTTENBERG is the author of *Surprised by God: How I Learned to Stop Worrying and Love Religion* (2008), editor of the anthologies *The Passionate Torah: Sex and Judaism* (2009) and *Yentl's Revenge: The Next Wave of Jewish Feminism* (2001), and coeditor of a series of forthcoming books on Jewish ethics. Her writing has appeared in a wide range of publications, and she is a contributing editor to the magazines *Lilith* and *Women and Judaism* as well as to the Web site Jewschool.com. She teaches and lectures nationwide, blogs at danyaruttenberg.net, and lives in the Boston area.

Acknowledgments

The creation of ritual objects rarely happens in a vacuum. Works are made for friends, family, or community. Artists create for an imagined set of users through the marketplace, trying to find homes for their designs around the world. Museums and other institutions invite artists to produce new work for exhibition, sale, or collection. Videos and other conceptual artworks about ritual depend very much on their participatory qualities. The process of reinvention depends on a prior establishment of a form of Judaica that is fundamentally communal.

In the same tradition, the process of creating this exhibition, and its accompanying catalogue, has been intensely collaborative. *Reinventing Ritual* was envisioned at The Jewish Museum long before my arrival in July 2007. It became my good fortune to take over the project, formulate criteria, and select and present the works. Joan Rosenbaum, the Helen Goldsmith Menschel Director of the Museum, and Ruth Beesch, Deputy Director for Program, have contributed powerful insights and tremendous support from the beginning, entrusting a complex show to a new curator, for which I am grateful.

The work of my predecessors—Fred Wasserman and Scott Ruby—expanded the Museum's holdings of and research into contemporary Judaica. Museum curators Susan Braunstein, Norman Kleeblatt, Claudia Nahson, and Orit Carmeli have enriched our conception of the field of ritual objects. Andrew Ingall and Alison Gass's research into "New Jew" art also served as a foundation. Mason Klein, Karen Levitov, Susan Goodman, Nelly Benedek, Aviva Weintraub, Joanna Montoya, Debbie Dorfman, and Stacey Zaleski each voiced opinions that contributed to the selection of works. Fred Wasserman, formerly Deputy Director of Programs at the Contemporary Jewish Museum in San Francisco, has been a wonderful collaborator as he has enthusiastically supported *Reinventing Ritual*. I thank Connie Wolf, director of the Contemporary Jewish Museum, and her staff for their involvement in this project.

The interpretation of contemporary Jewish ritual and art has taken several great leaps forward with the contributions of the essayists for the catalogue: Julie Lasky and Danya Ruttenberg. The pieces by Arnold M. Eisen and Joan Rosenbaum precisely calibrate the reinventions of ritual that have animated Jewish life in the past few decades, as well as the distinctive roles played by The Jewish Theological Seminary and The Jewish Museum. My essay was aided by Laurie Phillips, Susan Braunstein, and Norman Kleeblatt, whose close readings helped clarify the analysis. Mike Sittenfeld sagaciously directed the conceptualization and production of the catalogue, and Jenny Werbell fine-tuned the book and orchestrated myriad images. Emily Lessard has designed the intelligent, clear, and beautiful catalogue and exhibition graphics that we imagined. The team at Yale University Press, particularly Senior Editor Michelle Komie, ensured that this book would meet its high standards.

Curatorial program associates Tamar Rubin, Rachel Travis, and Melissa Klein managed with aplomb a million details for the exhibition and catalogue. Tamar's important contribution is present with the cultural timeline, Rachel's interpretative assistance has been indispensable, and Melissa handled the production of the exhibition video and labels. The exhibition benefitted immeasurably from the diligence of interns Alison Blanksteen and Emily Zandy, who provided outstanding organizational skills and bibliographic research.

Exhibition designer Adam Rolston is a man of many talents. His ideas about the forms of rituals and the rituals of exhibition led to a smart, coherent, and what I hope is an inspiring presentation of wide-ranging work. Thanks as well to Hilary Fulmer and the rest of the team at Incorporated. I am delighted that Adam Rolston and Emily Lessard independently arrived at the same design solution: an exhibition of diverse ritual art requires the symmetry and clarity of ritual itself. Robin White Owen of MediaCombo was instrumental in shaping the interpretive video.

The Jewish Museum operations, collections, and exhibitions team of Jane Rubin, Al Lazarte, Julie Maguire, Dolores Pukki, Elisabeth Manzi, Katherine Danalakis, Frank Sargenti, and Stacey Traunfeld ensured the smooth progress from a paper checklist to a complex, three-dimensional exhibition. They have anticipated and solved countless problems, making my job vastly simpler. The exhibition's appearance on the Web was spearheaded by Katharine Staelin. Publicity for the exhibition was handled superbly by Anne Scher and Alex Wittenberg.

Other curators and scholars working in the specialized area of contemporary Jewish ritual objects and art have generously shared knowledge and answered questions: Emily Bilski, director of the Adi Foundation, Jerusalem; Sharon Weiser-Ferguson, Judaica curator at the Israel Museum; Timna Seligman, Israeli art curator at the Israel Museum; Alex Ward, design curator at the Israel Museum; Staci Boris, curator at the Spertus Museum, Chicago; Alla Efimova, curator at the Judah L. Magnes Museum, Berkeley; Tal Gozani, curator at the Skirball Cultural Center, Los Angeles; Vivian B. Mann, professor at The Jewish Theological Seminary; Corey Wegener, curator at Minneapolis Institute of Arts; Edward van Voolen, curator at the Joods Historisch Museum, Amsterdam; Matthew Singer, curator at the Philadelphia Museum of Jewish Art; Laura Kruger, director of the museum of the Hebrew Union College-Jewish Institute of Religion, New York; Dara Solomon, curator at the Contemporary Jewish Museum; Maya Benton, curator at the International Center of Photography; and Rebecca Guber, director of the Six Points Fellowship, New York. Paul Zakrzewski of the Foundation for Jewish Culture and Dan Schifrin of the Contemporary Jewish Museum both kept me up to date on contemporary Jewish literature.

The Contemporary Judaica Acquisition Committee at The Jewish Museum is an ideal testing ground for new ideas and objects, and the committee's dedication and intelligence have contributed significantly to the rigor of the collection and exhibition. Chair Stuart Silver's visionary leadership of the creation of the committee and his ability to raise the bar and bring in substantial funding have been the backbone of the operation.

The Leir Charitable Foundations provided major financial support in the area of contemporary Jewish ritual art. From the endowing of a curatorial position at the Museum to providing travel funding, support for a prize, and commissions, the overarching Leir initiative at The Jewish Museum is a program that has taken the creation, exhibition, and interpretation of the rich interactions of art, design, and Jewish ritual into the twenty-first century.

Important loans for the exhibition were made possible by Steve Turner Contemporary, Los Angeles; Black and White Gallery, New York; Annely Juda Fine Art, London; P.P.O.W. Gallery, New York; Loushy Art & Projects, Tel Aviv; and Ronald Feldman Fine Arts, New York.

One's perspective on religious ritual often begins at home. My wife, Risa Kaufman, and daughter, Frieda Belasco, harmonize a life of intellectual and aesthetic inquiry in our community in Brooklyn, while my parents, Steve and Fran Belasco and Claire Eisenstadt and Sandy Bogin, bequeathed an amazing diversity of experiences of art and Jewish practice. My sister Judith Belasco, director of food programs at Hazon, introduced me to cutting-edge Jewish ritual and culture.

The artists in this exhibition all generously shared their processes, sources, fantasies, goals, anxieties, and of course brilliant work. Some have taken risks to contribute personal pieces in a context that is distinctly heterogeneous, so I am grateful for their trust. In addition, I would like to thank the many other artists, too numerous to name here, with whom I have had discussions in person, over the phone, or via e-mail in preparation for this exhibition. My role as curator has been, to paraphrase Ben Katchor, a middleman in the memory business.

DANIEL BELASCO
Henry J. Leir Assistant Curator
THE JEWISH MUSEUM

Index

Page numbers in boldface refer to illustrations

Aachen Passover Haggadah (Cherkassky), **101**

Abraham, Talila, *Dantela,* **xiv**, 14

Abrams, Rabbi Judith, 112n34

absorbing, 9, 15-28; internal process of, 15; learning via, 38; marriage as metaphor of, 24; and permeation of boundaries, 15

Abstract Expressionists, vii

Adilman, Rabbi Binyomin, 61, 114n5

Adler, Jonathan, *Utopia Menorah,* 32, **32**, 35

Adler, Rachel, *Engendering Judaism,* 112n38

aesthetics, relational, 3

Agam, Yaakov, and "metaphysical Judaica," 1

AgriProcessors, Postville, Iowa, 15

agunot (chained women), 27, 28

Akšamija, Azra, 82; *Frontier Vest,* 9, **10,** 79

Alchemy (Treister), 39, 40, **40**

Alef (album cover) (Masada), **95**

Alenikoff, Frances, 7

All Rise (Aylon), 44, 45, 79, 80, **80**

Alterman, Natan, 34

Ando, Tadao, 35

architecture: green, 47; sustainable, 47

Aron, Bill, *Hallel,* 72, **72**

art: and craftsmanship, 9; faith reinterpreted through, 7; interactive, 61; "post-identity," 9; ritual as medium of, 4-8

Artes Magnus, viii

Arts and Crafts movement, 73

Ashery, Oreet, *Dancing with Men,* 14, 90, **90**

Auslander, Sarah, and Johnathan Hopp, *Passover Plates,* 49, 56, **56,** 60-61

Avidan, Bruria, *Wedding Cup,* 24, 25, **25**

Aviv Yeshiva, Tel Aviv, 83

Aylon, Helène: 82, 112n36; *All Rise,* 44, 45, 79, 80, **80;** *The Liberation of G-d,* 44-45

Bal tashchit, 47, 49, 69, 114n5

bar mitzvah, 74

Barney, Carol Ross, 47

Bar Yochai, Rabbi Shimon, 90

bat mitzvah, 86

Batsry, Sahar, *Volcano Seder Plate,* **12-13,** 13, 14

Bazant, Micah, *TimTum,* 86, **87**

Beat poetry, 4, 5, 6

Bell, Catherine, 87

Benitez, Francisca, 49; *Sukkah,* 62, **62,** 63

Benow, Sheila, *The Happening,* 7, **7**

Berman, Wallace, 4-5; *Semina,* **4;** *Untitled,* **4**

Bible: as art medium, 38; sacredness of, 38

body: connection of mind and, 36; and covering, 15; as locus of religious experience, 7-8, 85-89

"bop kabbalah," 4

Bourriaud, Nicolas, 3

Boyarin, Daniel, 36

Boy George, 27, 28

Bresnick, Johanna, and Michael Cloud, *From Mouth to Mouth,* 38-39, 89, 91, **91,** 92

brit milah (circumcision), 85

building, 9, 28-36; creation of space in, 28, 34; destruction as creation, 34; and *eruv* (boundary line), 28; and menorahs, 35; and mezuzahs, 30, 31, 34-35; and repurposing, 35-36; sanctified settings, 28; unfinished eastern wall in, 29

Burks, Stephen, *Love Table,* 50, **50**

Cage, John, 4, 7

Calle, Sophie, *The Eruv of Jerusalem,* viii, 28

Canaday, John, 6

candles, lighting, 84
Canter, Alexis, *Wishbone*, 16, **16,** 22
Caporet (Rosenfeld), **54,** 55
Capuchin chapels, Rome, 53
Carlebach, Rabbi Shlomo, 7
Carnesky, Marisa, *Jewess Tattooess,* **97**
Catastrophe Vase (Velčovský), 52, **52**
CeMMent Mezuzah (Meisler), 31, **31,** 34
Chabad movement, 7
challah: covering of, 11; how to braid into a bird, 2, **2**
charity, and interactive art, 61
Cherkassky, Zoya: 112n36; *Aachen Passover Haggadah,* **100**
Choo, Chunghi, viii
Churban (destruction of the Temple), 29
Cliffs Notes, 65
Cloud, Michael, and Johanna Bresnick, *From Mouth to Mouth,* 89, 91, 92
Colbert, Stephen, *The Colbert Report,* **102**
Congregation Beth David, San Luis Obispo, 114n1
Congregation Emanu-El, San Francisco, 111n12
conspiracy theory, 41, 44
Content, Eli, viii
conversion rituals, 84
counterculture movement, 6
Cousineau, Jennifer, 28
covering, 9; and the concept of distinction, 11; and cross-dressing, 14; and new identity, 14;

prayer as ritual of, 11; relation of decorative and functional in, 14; rethinking one's garments, 14-15
craftsmanship, 9, 76
creation: gift of, 23; of the Jewish state, 34; and repurposing, 35-36
cross-dressing, 14

Dada, 44
Dairy and Meat Dishes (R. Moses), 18, **18**
Dancing with Men (Ashery), 14, 90, **90**
Dantela (Abraham), **xiv,** 14
Day Done (Landau), 28, 29, **29,** 34
DeFeo, Jay, *The Rose,* 4-5
Design Within Reach, 50, **50**
Deuteronomy, Book of, 116n6
Diamant, Anita, *The Red Tent,* **96**
Diaspora Judaism, 36
distinction, concept of, 11
"Do-It-Yourself," source of phrase, 73
Do-It-Yourself Charity Box (Wexler), 46, **46,** 47, 49, 57, **57,** 61
Drach, Ami, and Dov Ganchrow, *+/- Hotplate,* 19, **19,** 22
Dubowski, Sandi Simcha, *Trembling before G-d,* 9
Dybbuk, A, or Between Two Worlds (Kushner), **96**

Eisen, Arnold M., 8
Electric Blue/Shocking Pink (R. Moses), 18, **18**

Eliasson, Olafur, ix
Embrace (Mikesell), 35, 67, **67**
Enemy Kitchen (Rakowitz), 22
Engendering Judaism (R. Adler), 112n38
Eruv of Jerusalem, The (Calle), viii, 28
Esther, Book of, 39
Everything Is Illuminated (Foer), **100**
Exodus, 44
Ezekiel, Book of, 92

feminism, 7, 8, 44-45; and body as site of ritual, 86, **86;** in New Jewish ritual, 72, 73, 75-77, 79, 82, 86, 87; in Third Wave craft resurgence, 76
Fischer, R. M., 35
Foer, Jonathan Safran: *Everything Is Illuminated,* **100;** *If This Is Kosher . . . ,* 15
food: absorbing, 15; rituals for, 22, 24; *traif,* 22
Forman, Laura, 7
Freedom Seder, 6
Friedman, Idan, 51
Friedman, Jen Taylor, 75-76, **75**
Fringed Garment (Kanter), 11, 76, 77, **77**
Frishman, Rabbi Louis, 7
From Mouth to Mouth (Bresnick and Cloud), 38-39, 89, 91, **91,** 92
Frontier Vest (Akšamija), 9, **10,** 79
Frosine Glasses (Ivankovic), **60**

Galvanized Steel Candelabra (Grand), 33, **33**, 35

Ganchrow, Dov: and Ami Drach, *+/− Hotplate*, 19, **19**, 22; and Zivia, *Netilat Yadayim* (Hand Cleansing Vessel), 20, **20**, 22

Gardening Sukkah (Wexler), **58**, 59, **59**, 61, 63

gay and lesbian couples, Jewish commitment ceremonies of, 82

Geertz, Clifford, 84–85

Ginsberg, Allen, **6**; *Howl*, 4; *Kaddish*, 6

Godley, Lyn, viii

Golan, Nechama, 38; *Untitled*, 113n51

Goldstein, Rabbi Niles, 8

Goldvicht, Hadassa, *Writing Lesson #1*, 38, **70**, 81, **81**

Goodman, Louis, viii

Gore, Al, and Joe Lieberman, campaign button, **98**

Gottlieb, Adolph, 24

Gottlieb, Maurycy, 36

Grand, Joe, *Galvanized Steel Candelabra*, 33, **33**, 35

Grandma's Boy (Kaprow), 6

Grant, Deborah, 39; *(6 + 6 + 6 = 18 & 1 + 8 = 9) & 9 inverted is 6*, 41, **41**, 44

Griebel, Mila Tanya, *"Marriage, I would rather have a cup of tea!"* 27, **27**, 28

Halacha (Jewish law), 45

Hallel (Aron), 72, **72**

Handel, Steven N., and Mierle Laderman Ukeles, *"I'm Talking to You": A Scent Garden*, 23, **23**, 24

handicrafts, 2

Hanukkah lamps, 35

Happening, The (Benow), 7, **7**

happenings, 6

Hasidism, 7

Havdalah ritual, 23, 24, 85

Havurah movement, 72

Havurat Shalom, 6

Hazon Food Conference, 15, 112n35

Heeb magazine, **100**

Hekhsher Tzedek, 15

Heschel, Abraham Joshua, 82; *The Sabbath: Its Meaning for Modern Man*, 28

Hevruta-Mituta (Studio Armadillo), 38, 83, **83**

Highlights, 65

Hinkis, Tali, 28, 78

Hopp, Johnathan, and Sarah Auslander, *Passover Plates*, 49, 56, **56**, 60–61

Horowitz, Barbara, ix

Humane Kosher (web site), 15

If This Is Kosher . . . (Foer), 15

IKEA fabric, **54**, 55

"I'm Talking to You": A Scent Garden (Ukeles and Handel), 23, **23**, 24

Independent (London), 39, **40**

Ivankovic, Michelle, *Frosine Glasses*, **60**

Janco, Marcel, 110n10

Jewess Tattooess (Carnesky), **97**

Jewish action: being vs. doing, 8; counterculture movement, 6; feminism, 7, 8; Hasidism, 7; as ritual, 2–4; social justice, 8, 15; as source of contention, 6

Jewish Catalogue, The: A Do-It-Yourself Kit (Siegel et al., eds.), 2, **2**, 72–73, **73**, 76

Jewish Holiday Fun . . . for You! (Rushkoff), 69

Jewish practice, art of, 1–45; absorbing, 9, 15–28; building, 9, 28–36; covering, 9, 11, 14–15; exhibition as ritual, 8–15; Jewish action, 2–4; nature of, 1–2; precursors of, 4–8; thinking, 9, 36–45

Jewish practice, text-based, 36

Jewish Reconstructionist Congregation (JRC), Evanston, Illinois, 47, 48, **48**, 49, 50, 114n1

Jewish ritual, *see* New Jewish ritual; Ritual

Jewish state, creation of, 34

Jews and Shoes, 113n51

Johnson, Philip, AT&T (now Sony) Building, 52

Judaikitsch, 71

Kabbalat Shabbat service, 7

Kabbalists, 39, 74, 116n7

Kaddish, 84

Kahn, Boaz, 34

Kahn, Louis, 34

Kahn, Mey, 34

Kahn, Tobi, *Saphyr*, 43, **43,** 44

Kanof, Abram, vii

Kanter, Rachel, 14, 82; *Fringed Garment*, 11, 76, 77, **77**

kapparos (animal sacrifice), 74

Kaprow, Allan, 5–6; first Environment, **5**, 6; *Grandma's Boy*, 6

Karlsbad, Czechoslovakia, seder plate, 60, **60**

Kashrut, 15

Kaufmann, Isidor, 36

Kerouac, Jack, **6**

Ketubah (Rolling), 26, **26,** 28

Kingsley, Gershon, 7

Kligman, Barbara (Rushkoff), 65

Koresh, David (né Vernon Howell), 39, 44

Kosher Hot Dog Yarmulke, German Yarmulke, Stonewall Yarmulke, Swedish Yarmulke (Leibowitz), **96**

Kostianovsky, Tamara, *Unearthed*, 15, 17, **17**

Kruk, Hadas, 21, 83

Kushner, Tony, *A Dybbuk, or Between Two Worlds,* **96**

Lag b'Omer, 90

Landau, Sigalit, *Day Done,* 28, 29, **29,** 34

Lapidus, Kyle, 28, 78

Last Mikvah on Fifth Avenue, The (Romberg), viii

Lederman, Eran, and Elan Leor, *Solomon*, 30, 34

LEED (Leadership in Energy and Environmental Design) program, 47, **48,** 114n1

Leibowitz, Cary, *Kosher Hot Dog Yarmulke, German Yarmulke, Stonewall Yarmulke, Swedish Yarmulke,* **96**

Leor, Elan, and Eran Lederman, *Solomon*, 30, **30,** 34

Leviticus, Book of, 92

Liberation of G-d, The (Aylon), 44–45

Libeskind, Daniel, Jewish Museum Berlin, 38, **99**

Lieberman, Joe, and Al Gore, campaign button, **98**

"Lifting and saying," 21

Lissitzky, El, "Chad Gadya" illustrations, 110n10

List, Vera, vii, viii

Love Table (Burks), 50, **50**

LoVid, 28; *Retzuot (ShinShinAgam)*, 14, 78, **78**

marriage: commitment ceremonies, 82; life without, 27; as metaphor of absorption, 24; rituals of, 24, 28, 84; Seven Blessings of, 25; unification in, 24

"Marriage, I would rather have a cup of tea!" (Griebel), 27, **27,** 28

Marti, Virgil, *Untitled (Mezuzah),* 34, 49–50, **53**

Masada, *Alef* album cover, **95**

Matisyahu, *Shake Off the Dust . . . Arise* album cover, **101**

Matzdorf, Kurt, 39

Mayyim Hayyim mikvah, Newton, Massachusetts, **102**

Meesters, Jo, *Pulp*, 50, **50**

Megillat Esther (Waldman), 29, 93, **93**

Meier, Richard, *Recent American Synagogue Architecture,* viii

Meisler, Marit, *CeMMent Mezuzah*, 31, **31,** 34

Memphis movement, 52

Mendel, Rebbe Menachem of Kotzk, 114n5

Menorah (Reddish Studio), 35, 51, **51**

Menorahs, 35

MetalaceArt, 14

Mezuzahs: cases of, 34; *CeMMent Mezuzah,* 31, **31;** in demarcation of Jewish space, 34; protocols for, 53; *Rubble Fragment I,* 34, 49, 63, 65, 66, **66;** secular, 8; *Solomon,* 30, **30,** 34; *Untitled,* 34, 49–50, **53**

Michelin Guide, 65

Mikesell, Alix, 39; *Embrace,* 35, 67, **67;** *Sentinel,* 35, 67, **67**

mikvah, 86, **86, 102**

Milhaud, Darius, 111n12

Milk/Meat Couples (R. Moses), 18, **18**

"Miriam's cup," 115n4

Mishnah, compilation of, 36

mitzvah, "positive time-bound," 76

modernism, 55; music, 111n12; organic, 32

Moses, 114n5

Moses, Rachel, 22; *Dairy*

and Meat Dishes, 18, **18**; *Electric Blue/Shocking Pink*, 18, **18**; *Milk/Meat Couples*, 18, **18**
mourning rituals, 82, 84
Museum of Modern Art, 38
Myerhoff, Barbara G., 2
My Mexican Shivah (Springall), **103**

Neo-Dada, 4
Netilat Yadayim (Ganchrow and Zivia), 20, **20**, 22
New Jewish ritual, xi-xiii, 71-93; ambiguity in, 87; as beyond language, 85-86; body as site for, 85-89; and cultural tolerance, 82; do-it-yourself, 72-74, 76; feminist, 72, 73, 75-77, 79, 82, 86, 87; havurah movement, 72; internal-izing Torah, 89, 91, **91**, 92; on multiple planes, 84-85, 87; prayer as worship, 74; and religious identity, 82; and social change, 82, 84-85
Newman, Barnett, 1; *Stations of the Cross*, **5**, 6
New York Havurah, 72
Nivinsky, Ignaty, *The Golem* designs, 110n10

Ochs, Vanessa, 3
Octogenarian (Smulovitz), 37, **37**, 39
Omer, 42, 43, 44
Opshernish (Waxman), 87, 88, **88**, 89
Orthodox communities, 8, 38, 45
ossuaries, 34

Otterness, Tom, viii
Otterson, Joel, 35

Paris, Norm, *Rubble Fragment I (Mezuzah)*, 34, 49, 63, 65, 66, **66**
Park Avenue Synagogue, New York, 111n12
Parokhet (Rosenfeld), 49, 54, **54**, 55
Passover: Christian seders, 8; and the Exodus, 44; politically conscious celebrations of, 6; popularity of, 60; "seder in the streets," 82
Passover Plates (Hopp and Auslander), 56, **56**, 60-61
Perloff, Marjorie, 4
Plaskow, Judith, 7
Plotz zine (Rushkoff), 49, 65, 68, **68**, 69
+/− Hebrew (Drach and Ganchrow), 19, **19**, 22
Polish Wooden Synagogues (Stella), viii
Pollan, Michael, 24
Pop Art, 57
postmodernism, 52
prayer: and covering, 11; as proper worship, 74; as substitute for sacrifice, 116n6
Presley, Elvis, 52
Pulp (Meesters), 50, **50**
Purim, and Book of Esther, 39

rabbinical Judaism, 36, 74
Rakowitz, Michael, *Enemy Kitchen*, 22
Rashid, Karim, viii
reconstruction, 9
recontamination, avoidance of, 20

recycling, 47-69; and adaptability, 69; and *bal tashchit*, 47, 49, 69; and conservation, 49-50; in context, 52; of fragments, 63, 65; and green architecture, 47; old materials in new forms, 49, 63; and personification, 49; and preservation, 69; and sustainability, 52, 69; Talmudic examples of, 55; and *tikkun olam* (repairing the world), 48; and usefulness, 69
Reddish Studio, *Menorah*, 35, 51, **51**
Red Tent, The (Diamant), **96**
Reform Jewish architec-ture, 32
Reform movement, 8
relational aesthetics, 3
repurposing, 35-36. *See also* recycling
Retzuot (ShinShinAgam) (LoVid), 14, 78, **78**
ritual: as Jewish action, 2-4; as medium of art, 4-8; new, *see* New Jewish ritual; as open system, 4, 87; and ritualism, 6; sexism in, 44
Rolling, Tracy, *Ketubah*, 26, **26**, 28
Romberg, Oswaldo, *The Last Mikvah on Fifth Avenue*, viii
Rosenberg, Harold, 1-2, 36
Rosenfeld, Galya, 60; *Caporet*, **54**, 55; *Parokhet*, 49, 54, **54**, 55
Rose, The (DeFeo), 4-5
Rosh Chodesh, 73

Ross Barney Architects, *Jewish Reconstructionist Congregation*, 47, 48, **48,** 49, 50

Rothfarb, Shari, *Water Rites*, viii

Rothko, Mark, 1, 24

Rubber Tubs (Slizewicz), 50, **50**

Rubble Fragment I (Mezuzah) (Paris), 34, 49, 63, 65, 66, **66**

Rushkoff, Barbara: *Jewish Holiday Fun . . . for You!* 69; *Plotz* zine, 49, 65, 68, **68,** 69

Rushkoff, Douglas, 8

Sabbath, The: Its Meaning for Modern Man (Heschel), 28

Sandqvist, Tom, 110n10

Saphyr (Kahn), 43, **43,** 44

Sarna, Jonathan D., 8

"Save the Rebbe's Home" button, **95**

Schneerson, Rabbi Menachem Mendel, **95**

Secession style, 39

seder plate, Czechoslovakia, 60, **60**

Seder Plate (Studio Armadillo), 21, **21**

seders: Christian, 8; Freedom, 6; "in the streets," 82

Sefer ha-Chinuch, 49

Segal, Arthur, 110n10

Seinfeld (TV), 65

Semicha (rabbinical ordination), 45

Semina (Berman), 4

Sentinel (Mikesell), 35, 67, **67**

Sephirot (ten attributes of God), 39

Sephirot Haomer (Wilner), 42, **42,** 44

Shahn, Ben, "metaphysical Judaica" of, 1

Shake Off the Dust . . . Arise (album cover) (Matisyahu), **101**

Shavuot, first night of, 44

Siegel, Richard, 2, 73

Sieradski, Daniel, 82; *Tallit Katan Shel Shabbatai Tzvi,* 79, **79,** 82

Singer, Matthew, 113n45

(6 + 6 + 6 = 18 & 1 + 8 = 9) & 9 inverted is 6 (Grant), 41, **41,** 44

Slizewicz, Thaddée de, *Rubber Tubs,* 50, **50**

Smulovitz, Anika: *Octogenarian,* 37, **37,** 39; *Untitled,* 37, **37,** 39

Sottsass, Ettore, Carlton room divider, 52

Spertus Institute, Chicago, 112n30

Springall, Alejandro, *My Mexican Shivah,* **103**

Stations of the Cross (Newman), **5,** 6

Stein, Anat, 21, 83

Steinbock, Naama, 51

Stella, Frank, *Polish Wooden Synagogues,* viii

Strassfeld, Michael, 2, 73

Strassfeld, Sharon, 2, 73

Studio Armadillo, 22, 36; *Hevruta–Mituta,* 38, 83, **83;** *Seder Plate,* 21, **21**

Studio Museum in Harlem, 112n30

Sukkah (Benitez), 49, 62, **62,** 63

sukkahs, viii, **58,** 59, **59,** 61–63

sustainability, 52, 69

Swartz, Julianne, ix

Tabernacle, 11

tallit (prayer shawl), 11, 75–76, 77, **77,** 79, **79**

tallit katan (fringed garment), 75–76, 79

Tallit Katan Shel Shabbatai Tzvi (Sieradski), 79, **79,** 82

Talmud, compilation of, 36

Taragan, Liora, 49, 50; *Wedding Dress,* 63, 64, **64**

tashlich (casting bread into the water), 74

tefillin (phylacteries), 11, 14, 78

Temple Beth El, Spring Valley, New York, Shabbat "art service" in, 7, **7**

Temple Beth Shalom, San Francisco, 113n44

Temple Israel, Greenfield, Massachusetts, viii

Temple Judaism, 36

Temple of Jerusalem, 29, 35, 36

thinking, 9, 36–45; and the act of counting, 44; and creativity, 39; mind-body connection, 36; and religious education, 38

thkines, Ashkenazi women's, 74

Tihany, Adam, viii

tikkun olam (repairing the world), 48

TimTum (Bazant), 86, **87**

Torah: celebration of, 36; comic book of, 93, **93;** covering of, 11; debate of, 36; internalizing gastronomically, 89, 91, **91,** 92; metaphor of, 24; multiple authors of, 39; new interpretations of, 82; sanctity of, 38; study of, 89

Torah pointer (*yad*), 37, 38-39

transgression, fear of, 18

Treister, Suzanne, *Alchemy,* 39, 40, **40**

Trembling before G-d (Dubowski), 9

Tu BiShvat seder, 74

Tzara, Tristan, 110n10

tzedakah boxes, 57, **57,** 61, 72

tzitzit (fringes), 11, 75-76, **75, 77,** 79

Ukeles, Mierle Laderman, and Steven N. Handel, *"I'm Talking to You": A Scent Garden,* 23, **23,** 24

Unearthed (Kostianovsky), 15, 17, **17**

Untitled (Berman), **4**

Untitled (Golan), 113n51

Untitled (Smulovitz), 37, **37,** 39

Untitled (Mezuzah) (Marti), 34, 49-50, 53, **53**

U.S. Green Building Council, LEED program, 47, **48,** 114n1

Utopia Menorah (J. Adler), 32, **32,** 35

Velčovský, Maxim, *Catastrophe Vase,* 52, **52**

Victorian fashion, 63

Vignelli, Lella, viii

Viola, Bill, 86

Volcano Seder Plate (Batsry), **12-13,** 13, 14

Waldman, JT, *Megillat Esther,* 39, 93, **93**

Wallinger, Mark, 38

Warhol, Andy, Campbell's Soup can, 57

Waskow, Arthur, 73

Water Rites (Rothfarb), viii

Waxman, Lori, 22

Waxman, Tobaron, *Opshernish,* 87, 88, **88,** 89

Weber, Max, 36

Wedding Cup (Avidan), 24, 25, **25**

Wedding Dress (Taragan), 63, 64, **64**

Weill, Kurt, 111n12

Wexler, Allan: *Do-It-Yourself Charity Box,* 46, **46,** 47, 49, 57, **57,** 61; *Gardening Sukkah,* viii, **58,** 59, **59,** 61, 63; mezuzahs, viii

wigs, women's head-covering, 116n5

Williamsburg, Brooklyn, sukkahs in, 49, 62, **62,** 63

Wilner, Martin, *Sephirot Haomer,* 42, **42,** 44

Wishbone (Canter), 16, **16,** 22

Writing Lesson #1 (Goldvicht), 38, **70,** 81, **81**

"Yedid Nefesh" (medieval poem), 89

Yoshino, Kenji, 112n32

Young, LaMonte, 7

Zabari, Moshe, viii

Zivia, and Dov Ganchrow, *Netilat Yadayim,* 20, **20,** 22

138